Sweet Honesty

The Beverley Martyn Story

by

Beverley Martyn

**Grosvenor House
Publishing Limited**

This book is published by
Grosvenor House Publishing Ltd
28-30 High Street, Guildford, Surrey, GU1 3HY.
www.grosvenorhousepublishing.co.uk

A CIP record for this book
is available from the British Library

ISBN 978-1-907211-88-1

To my parents and friends who have gone before
...and 'thank you' to Jaki for being so patient!

Thanks also to Ewen, Deborah, Lucy, Roger and Amber for their help and support.

Contents

PROLOGUE – *Heathfield February 1979*

John held the handle of the carving knife against my breastbone and pressed himself against the point.

"Go on, kill me. You'd love to, wouldn't you?" he slurred in that thick Glaswegian accent of his that emerged every time he had too much drink or drugs.

"Leave her, John, leave her!" Hamish Imlach was in the front room, witnessing this display of domestic violence.[1] I was already reeling from where John had been banging my head against the meat hooks hanging in our kitchen, probably because I looked at him wrongly, and I shot a look at Hamish, silently begging him to get me out of this. "Stop it John!" he came to my aid, "That's enough." John let the knife go. "Get up to bed", he snarled at me and walked back to join our guest of the night.

Get up to bed? In my own house? In that instance something finally snapped in me. What was I, a child, or a grown woman and the mother of this man's children? All I had done to provoke this attack was to say I was too tired to serve a meal to these two men on their return from a night in the pub. As I got to my feet and left the room, I knew in that moment I either had to get out of this relationship, or one of us would be dead, and it would probably be me.

I was barefoot, so I quietly slipped my feet into a pair of my oldest son's boots and let myself out of the front door.

---

[1] **Hamish Imlach** (1940-1996) Legendary Scottish folk singer and raconteur, a major influence on John Martyn and Billy Connelly among many others.

I ran. I ran down the path and out into the dark street. It was like a dream I'd been having over and over in which I was silently screaming, running away from something fearful, something that was John. I knew I had become a piece of nothing, a wrung out rag. I was too exhausted by the madness of ten years of this marriage to fight back. I could do nothing but leave my children sleeping in their beds and flee into the night.

Heathfield is a small country town, there were no street lights every few yards, no phone box on every corner. I ran as fast as I could. I thought I could hear John coming after me; it's true what they say - fear gave me wings. I ran to the local police station but it was shut that time of night. And then I saw a car. I ran into the road and frantically waved it down. "Please help me. I need to get to the police but there's no-one at the station."

The driver was a nice man who took me to a phone box where I called the police and then he waited with me until they arrived. The police were kind, they came and put a coat round my shoulders and told me I had to go back to the house or John could have me for deserting the children. There wasn't much they could do in practice but they helped me understand my rights; domestic violence wasn't the issue in those days it is now. But I couldn't bring myself to go straight back. I went first to a friend's house and then to a solicitor.

So began the process of extricating myself from ten years of an abusive, destructive marriage that had stripped me of everything, from my self-confidence to my career. All the hopes and dreams I had nurtured as a child, all the promise of my youth had been ground to dust by this man. It was as if John Martyn had built his career on my bones. How can a woman let this happen to her? Was there something dark in John, something that made him a user and abuser for his own selfish ends? Or was it all my own fault, my own stupidity? How, oh how had it come to this?

CHAPTER 1

Coventry – London 1947-1962

Post-war Coventry 1947. The city had been ravaged by Luft-waffe bombing in 1940 and still bore the scars, but amid the rubble and bomb damage life went on and I was born on March 24ᵗʰ, the child of first generation Polish/Jewish immi-grants. There were five children in our family, four girls and a boy and I was somewhere in the middle, although my youngest sister didn't arrive until I was eleven or twelve. I have always thought of myself as English, born here, brought up among English people in a place where there were only just enough Jewish families to make up the congregation for a synagogue. We were the only Jewish kids on our block, and that made my heritage something alien to me.

My parents weren't a well-matched couple. My father wanted a traditional wife, someone to cook and clean and keep the house tidy but she was of a different calibre; she was highly intelligent, well-read and a great communicator. This led to conflict between them. I loved her deeply and she inspired me with her intellect and her love, whereas he frightened me with his anger and coldness towards me and his violence towards her. He seemed to bring a darkness into the house with him all the time. I was afraid of him and the fights he would have with my mother.

I remember one early incident when we children were woken during the night by the noises coming from downstairs. My older sister and I decided to investigate because we were worried about mum, scared that she might be in danger. I must have been about three or four and my sister seven. When we got downstairs, both my parents were there and we saw that mum had blood all over her face. My memory is that my sister snatched up the bread knife, pointed it at my father's stomach and said: "If you ever touch her again, I'll kill you!" And she meant it.

It wasn't a good thing for small children to see, this domestic violence, but it ran like a thread through my childhood. For years I didn't sleep properly because my father would be ranting and smashing things up. I was terrified of him and of what he would do to my mother, so I would hover on the edge of sleep all night, then doze off in school during the day. I didn't understand my father's nervousness.

Looking back, I suppose that any adult Jew who lived through the Second World War must have felt nervous, but I thought of myself as an English child and all I could see was that I had a father who was different from the other children's fathers. We children didn't know what bad memories he carried inside him, didn't understand what it meant to be a first generation immigrant, to have lost everything when the family had to flee persecution.

My paternal grandfather had come to this country with a reel of cotton and a needle and, like so many of his fellow émigrés, he had built a business from those small beginnings. Nobody talked about the past and you don't think about things like that when you're growing up. We had no idea what effect that sort of experience had on a man and my father certainly never opened up to me about his past. Nor did he ever talk to a shrink or a counsellor, as far as I know. Wrong generation. But that's what destroys people, keeping all the bad things inside.

The first house I remember we lived in was a little two-up-two-down next to a bombsite. There was no hot running water; there was an outside toilet and we had to go to the public baths when we needed a good wash. Looking back, I suppose you would have called it a slum, but the people around were lovely and as children we felt safe playing in the streets, even if we didn't have money for luxuries. Rationing was still in place for sweets, for clothes, for meat even, and we often lived on stews made from a scrap of meat with lentils or vegetables.

Vegetables were quite plentiful then because many people were still growing food in their gardens, although flowers were beginning to be planted again. There was beauty too. In the midst of all the destruction, the bombsites flowered and became places of magic and mystery. The people in the house next to ours even kept chickens in their garden! We would wake in the mornings to a *cockle doodle doo*. That was wonderful in the middle of a city.

But life was hard for my mother, especially the winters, which I remember as really cold, freezing. We could never afford to heat the whole house, so life tended to centre on the one room. There was only ever a fire upstairs if one of us was ill. Downstairs everything was focussed on the black range. It gave us heat and warm food; you could cook on it and dry your clothes in front of it at the same time. We had a front room, but that was rarely heated, so I remember it always smelled a bit damp and the books that were kept in there turned yellow.

Looking back, I realise my mother was worked to death. Five children generated a lot of washing and it would take all day. There were no disposable nappies either, everything had to be boiled. There was a copper in the back yard and a mangle, no washing machines or laundrettes in those days. If my mother needed to do a wash she had to start by going out to search for coal and then boiling the water. For a woman it meant drudgery, day in and day out. For a child, it meant you had to learn pretty early to become self-sufficient a lot of the time or you would be just adding to her problems.

But in spite of the hardships, I remember those years as a happy time, aside from my father.

I started school at the nearby Church of England primary school. My first acting role was there and it was as Mary in the nativity play. I had to take a note home asking my mother if it was all right for me to play the mother of Jesus. "Of course," she said, "Mary was a Jewish girl!" I was still confused about Jews and Christians. But none of that mattered when my big day came. I threw my hands in the air, like a silent movie star, as Gabriel came to make his annunciation and I delivered my line: "Behold the handmaid of the Lord!" Everyone said I was a natural, that I had *it*. That was the beginning of my love of performance, of theatre. I had dreams and hopes. I would succeed and rescue my mother from the harshness of her life. One day...

Being Jewish, we eventually had to start going to the synagogue. I didn't *feel* Jewish, I felt English, but it was part of our life and had to be addressed. And to others we were outsiders, whether we had been born in this country or not. I had my share of racial abuse over the years. When I was about five or six, Asian immigrants began to move into the area and because I used to go very dark in the summer, the local kids would ask me if I were a 'Paki'. When I replied I was a Jew they'd shout back: "You killed Jesus!" to which I'd retort: "No, I didn't! I wasn't there!" So I wasn't that comfortable about going to the synagogue. I was English, I had been assimilated into English culture and wanted to be like everybody else. But I had to go for a while until I had a strange experience that put me off forever.

I have always been something of a mystic. When I was little, I started to have these strange dreams about wooden poles, dreams that frightened me. What were these poles? I talked to my parents about it and my father asked if I were talking about Polish people. My mother knew I didn't mean people but even she couldn't explain them to me.

I used to have to be comforted at night when these dreams came upon me. Somehow, through the years, although no-one could explain them to me, I instinctively felt they had something to do with religion. I finally discovered their meaning many years later. I now know I was dreaming about Asherah, the Hebrew goddess.[2] You won't find her mentioned by name in many versions of the Bible, but I'm sure the rabbis knew of her existence.

I don't know whether my father talked to anyone at the synagogue about me and my dreams, but just before I reached puberty, he took me there one Sunday and went off and left me alone there with three rabbis, who seemed to be doing some sort of ritual, some magic. It seemed very weird to me, almost sinister, and I really didn't like it. I went home and told my mother I wasn't going to the synagogue again.

Things changed for the better when I was about eight or nine. Dad had learned how to be a watchmaker and his little business suddenly started to take off. That led to our moving to a bigger and better house in a smarter neighbourhood. I don't know whether it was because he got in with the Jewish equivalent of the Freemasons, or because he had begun playing table-tennis for the local Binley team. Whatever the reason, we were all very happy. Now we had not only an indoor bathroom – luxury of luxuries – we had an enormous garden to play in; I thought we'd moved to paradise.

We children had our own little playhouse out back with a parquet floor and its own sink, and we'd hold parties there and act out little plays for our friends. Best of all, there was a quarry at the bottom of the garden that seemed like the Grand Canyon to us. You could scoot down the clay sides on your arse and at the bottom there were ponds filled with newts and frogs. I would spend hours trying to catch the newts so I could take them home and watch their legs grow. I remember long

---

[2]**Asherah.** Consort of YHWH (Yahweh/Jehovah). Her name is usually translated in the Bible as 'poles', referring to the wooden poles that were erected in her honour. An 8th century BCE inscription linking her name with Yahweh's was unearthed in the Sinai in 1975. See Raphael Patai : 'The Hebrew Goddess' Wayne University Press (1990).

summer days that seemed to last forever because we were never in the house in the daylight hours. Butterflies danced everywhere... I remember being so happy in that house in St. Paul's Road that it even encouraged me to do well at school; it was at this time that I started reading well, but it hadn't always been like that.

I had been having problems at school. Everyone said how bright I was but how I was also dreamy. They didn't understand that when I was staring out of the window I was creating in my mind. I was also so shy that my mother nicknamed me Mouse. My first school had been in the poorer part of Coventry and the teachers there had been rather ancient. I remember my mother once going to complain because I started calling Kellogg's cornflakes 'Kelloyys'. She couldn't understand why I had developed such an odd habit until she talked to my teacher and discovered that the old dear had taught it to us like that because the 'g's in the name on the packet weren't joined up so she'd assumed they were 'y's!

My biggest problem was with numbers. I suffered from dyscalculia, a sort of number dyslexia, and I used to get into a terrible state before any maths test. I would do well in everything else, but my maths always let me down. And there was no-one to help me. My mother did her best, but she was a battered wife with a million and one things to do, and my father never showed any interest in me anyway. That, coupled with my fear of him and my years of disturbed sleep meant that when I came to take the eleven plus, I just couldn't handle the maths and I didn't get into grammar school. I was devastated. I felt like a reject, a second class child. I would have to go to the secondary modern. Children's futures were decided with no account taken of their home lives or what they'd been through. I seemed to have lost my future almost before it began. But then a man named Neil Stair came into my life and turned everything around.

Men have always played an important part in my life. Probably too important. I've trusted them when I shouldn't have done and leaned on them when I should have leaned on myself. I suppose when your father isn't there for you, when he lets you down, it leaves you vulnerable. You don't know who to trust, who are the good guys and who the bad. But when you're young and at the height of your beauty, there are always men attracted to you and it's easy to misread their messages. I think I was desperate for male attention, desperate for a man who would be there for me. Neil seemed to be that man and for the next four years he filled the void left by my father's indifference.

Neil became the drama teacher at the secondary modern school I was sent to and it was as if he zoomed in on me as soon as we met; he became my mentor. He told me I was special, that I had a real talent and I fell under his spell immediately. He told me I was beautiful and had the gift of words. He gave me praise when my father never had, took an interest in how I looked. He encouraged me to grow my hair long and even suggested the sort of eye make-up I should use. He became like a replacement father for me. I craved his attention because my dad seemed to have so little time for anyone in the family.

To a twelve-year-old girl, Neil was a fantastic figure. He was young and cultured, he knew about fine art, about music, about everything. He was a bohemian and a gentleman in every sense of the word, good-looking and graceful. He even smelled beautiful and he dressed exquisitely. And he was safe; I wasn't terrified of him like I was of my father and I blossomed under his tutelage.

When he chose me to play the part of a Japanese prince in a play we were entering in some drama festivals, I really felt I had become somebody. We won first prize in the Nuneaton and Leamington Spa drama festivals and I loved every minute of it. I was good at playing a boy, I was boyish-looking, I had a *gamin* face and no tits to speak of yet. The next year we won again, this time with me playing Ruth from the biblical story.

Suddenly I felt I had clout, I hadn't dropped through the net and got lost among the also-rans. Neil encouraged me to apply for drama school and even took me for an audition to the Royal

Shakespeare Company when I was about fourteen because they were looking for fairies for a production of 'A Midsummer Night's Dream'.

By the time the audition came through, however, I had grown into someone who looked more like Joan of Arc than Peasblossom. I wasn't suitable any longer for that production but I was told I had an exceptional talent and the directors of the RSC would write to my local council themselves to recommend me for a grant so I could attend drama school. Roy Dotrice was one of the people who auditioned me and he encouraged me to apply for the Corona Academy of Theatre Arts in London, the same school his daughters were attending.[3] I was on cloud nine and Neil had done this for me. Of course I was in love with him; I thought he was the love of my life. He had been my Svengali, my Professor Higgins, and I adored him.[4] But at fifteen I turned into a woman, and my castle in the air came crashing down.

As soon as my breasts began to develop it was as if I lost all of my power. Neil began to criticise me, to put my work down, to drive me to tears. When I started wearing a bra he would say things like: "What's that bra you're wearing? It's not very good, you know. You look like a letter S." It's hurtful stuff to a teenage girl. I couldn't understand the change in him. I thought it had to be my fault, that there was something wrong with me. I became anorexic, trying to stop the changes in my body. I thought he didn't love me anymore because I wasn't thin enough. And then my mother told me the truth – he was homosexual.

---

[3] **Roy Dotrice** (b1925) Well respected British actor. Father of Michele, who is best remembered as Betty, Frank Spencer's wife in 'Some Mothers Do 'Ave 'Em (1973-1978) and real life wife of the late Edward Woodward. Her mother Kay and sisters Karen and Yvette were also actors.

[4] **Svengali** - The evil hypnotist from Georges du Maurier's novel 'Trilby' (1894). **Professor Higgins** - Eliza Doolittle's mentor in George Bernard Shaw's play 'Pygmalion' (1913), better known today as the musical 'My Fair Lady'.

To say I was devastated is to put it mildly. I had built so many dreams on this man; I'd believed he loved me as I loved him and that this was like courtly love and first love all rolled into one. And then just at the point I was becoming a woman, he rejected me. Perhaps I was lucky he hadn't been a paedophile who took advantage of my naivety but that didn't stop it hurting. I was fifteen, about to move south on my own to enrol in drama school and heart-broken; I was distraught. And as if that all wasn't enough, my father was blaming me for the financial difficulties the family was now facing as a result of my application for a grant. It wasn't the most auspicious way to take on London.

CHAPTER 2

London 1962-1966

Whatever they tell you about the '60s, they were a terrific time to be young, even if you were as poor as a church mouse. We had opportunities our parents and grandparents could only dream of. A good education was there for anyone to take advantage of – university, art college, drama school, they were all freely available for those with the talent and the will. If your family had limited funds, you could apply for a grant. The only problem was that your parents' financial status had to be investigated as part of the process. By this time, my dad had two shops and seemed to be making a decent enough living, but we weren't wealthy. We were comfortable, in a nice house, but I still qualified for a state aid, so I applied. What none of my family realised was that my father was addicted to gambling and he was out of control.

He was spending more than he was making and he just wouldn't face what was going on. My mother tried to make him do his books for the accountant, but he ignored her. He hadn't paid any taxes for years, so when I applied for the grant, it all came out into the open and he was ruined and had to declare bankruptcy.

He blamed me for what happened and I don't think he ever forgave me. If he had been indifferent to me before, now he was downright hostile, saying things like he wished I'd never been born. It was a hard thing to bear when all I craved was his love and attention. To make matters worse, as I was leaving for

London, the family had to move out of our beautiful house and Mum was reduced once again to a squalid existence. It was the end of their marriage.

I'm sure my mother never said: "I told you so" to him; she wasn't like that. She had done her best to make a life with this man who would come home in a dark mood night after night and smash up everything in the house, but their relationship couldn't survive this. So the marriage ended.

He moved into a bachelor pad of some sort, and my mum had to go back to a two-up-two-down slum area. I don't think he even provided for her after their break-up but I wasn't really sure about what was happening in Coventry. I was pushing off to London, to my new life, and to be honest, I didn't really want to know what was happening in the world I'd left behind me. I only saw my father a few times again before he died in the 1980s and, much to my regret, we never did build a loving relationship.

You can be so selfish when you are fifteen, thinking the world revolves around you and you've got to get in there and show everyone just how beautiful and talented you are. I had been offered my chance at grabbing the brass ring, and I was going to take it.[5] Then I could rescue my mother from her misery. Life always ends in a happy-ever-after, doesn't it? At fifteen I never dreamt it could be different.

Mum took me down to London herself. I was very young to be starting at drama school so I had to be boarded with this couple from Cheshire, their two daughters and the grandmother. It wasn't the happiest place to start. For one thing, they kept making me big breakfasts, full of bacon, which they urged me to eat. Were they trying to convert me? For another, they were incredibly snobbish and unhip and kept trying to make me change the sort of clothes I wore.

---

[5]Grabbing the brass ring - the chance of winning a prize, from the early days of a carousel ride.

In the '60s the young were developing their own sense of fashion for the first time ever, really. No more dressing like miniature adults, the world was our oyster and we could pick and choose our pearls. From Mary Quant to Granny Takes a Trip we chose what was comfortable for us and created our own look.[6] I didn't have a lot of money to spare, so I went for the beatnik, bohemian look. I would go to college in jeans, duffle coat and a college scarf thrown round my neck.

It seemed that my hosts were embarrassed by having this trendy-looking bird traipsing up their stairwell, and after they'd asked me three times to dress differently, I felt it was time to move on. Fortunately, there was a good friend of my family's living in Maida Vale and she let me stay with her. I was also lucky to have my Aunt Madie living in London. She was delighted that one of her brother's kids was making something of herself and was kind enough to treat me to the sort of accessories a poor drama student really needed but couldn't afford, like a foil for fencing classes, or the right sort of tights from Frederick Freed's.[7]

It was hard work at drama school, but I loved it. At first I couldn't understand why we had to bother with things like dance and movement - I wanted to be a *serious* actress, not a jazz ballet dancer - but gradually I realised that toning the whole body is crucial for an actor, whatever role they play. You need confidence in your body and suppleness; you need to know how to carry yourself on stage or TV, whether you're in Shakespeare or Eastenders. Acting is a craft as well as an art, and they were training us to be professionals.

We'd exercise three or four hours a day and I discovered I had rhythm; I could dance with the best of them, even though I wasn't that interested. And there were some very good

---

[6]**Mary Quant** (b1934) Seminal dress designer of the '60s. Credited with popularising the mini skirt. **Granny Takes a Trip** - Famous vintage clothes boutique opened on Chelsea's King's Road, London 1966.

[7]**Freed of London Ltd** (est.1928) Makers of ballet shoes and associated gear.

students at Corona in those days – Richard O'Sullivan, Fraser Hines, Dennis Waterman, Francesca Annis, Susan Tracy – we were a core group of serious actors and we bonded well together, even though I was younger than the rest of them.[8]

Of course there were other students, *wannabes* with no talent but rich fathers, and some could be bitchy as hell. But I had my group, my friends, and I adored it. I was doing well too. I got my first TV part while still a student, in an episode of 'Dixon of Dock Green', playing a runaway art student. Jane Asher was the main guest star of the production but I don't remember ever getting to talk to her. She was in the middle of her big romance with Paul McCartney, and that put her on a different planet to the rest of us mere mortals![9]

I was still at drama school when I started singing in the folk clubs that were then mushrooming around London. When you're young, you have all the energy in the world. I'd work like a dog at Corona's during the day, then take off for Soho in the evenings to hang out with all these cool musicians. There was the 100 Club and Les Cousins in Greek Street. Everyone went there at the weekends. Performers such as Davey Graham and Donovan would get up and do a set, and any Americans passing through town would stop by for a visit.[10] The atmosphere was terrific. Folk and blues were coming alive in the Sixties. I went to see the great Pete Seeger play at the Unity Theatre near Euston.[11] My mother had been a member of the Unity when she was young and I was curious to see this place that had

---

[8]All these actors achieved successful careers, especially on television.

[9] **Jane Asher** (b1946) English actress who was engaged to Paul McCartney from 1967-1968. She later married Gerald Scarfe, the cartoonist, and is now best known for her cake decorations. **Sir Paul McCartney** (b1942) Founder member of The Beatles and still going strong.

[10]**Davey Graham** (1940-2008) Influential British folk guitarist of the '60s. **Donovan** (b1946) Very successful Scottish singer/songwriter.

[11]**Pete Seeger** (b1919) Iconic American folk singer/songwriter and activist. The **Unity Theatre** flourished from 1936-1983.

the reputation of being a Communist theatre. The old order was passing away. Tin Pan Alley no longer held the monopoly on popular music.[12] The Beatles were writing their own songs and there was a hunger for new artists with original material.

It really was a working class revolution; kids from families whose voices had never been heard before were creating art and poetry and getting paid for it; Angry Young Men had been writing plays that electrified a generation; we went on Ban the Bomb marches and really thought we could save the world. My god, it was an exhilarating time to be young and in London! We were the first generation after the war, and we had the time, space and money enough to be able to think about what war really meant. I think our parents were jealous of us in a way.

They had grown up being dictated to by their parents, then had to face the horror of war, and here we were enjoying an undreamt-of freedom, challenging all the traditions and taboos that had shaped their experience. There was a spiritual revolution going on too. The religions we'd grown up with could no longer be trusted. For many, God had died in the gas chambers of Auswitchz; the traditional institutions had no answers for the questions we were asking. It was a time of exploration. Yes, there was sex and drugs and rock 'n' roll, but there was also the protest song, the turning towards the East for spiritual guidance, the turning within to find our own truths.

I started my singing career by hanging out at the National Gallery on a Sunday evening with a bunch of bohemians that included Iron Foot Jack, Ian Dury and a load of art teachers and students.[13] We'd go to Finch's pub in Soho to drink cheap

---

[12]**Tin Pan Alley.** Nickname of Denmark Street, London, the centre of the UK music business. Originally referring to an area in New York that became the first major centre of popular music publishing c1885.

[13]**Iron Foot Jack.** Self-styled 'King of the Bohemians' and a regular character in Soho in the '50s and '60s. Long haired, sporting a swirling black cape and an iron boot, he would attempt to sell his poems to unwitting passers-by. **Ian Dury** (1942-2000) Music legend and founder of Ian Dury and the Blockheads.

white wine, then move on to the folk clubs. I met Don Partridge when he was busking one day near the National Gallery, at the bottom of Charing Cross Road.[14] I stopped to listen to him playing the blues and suddenly he thrust a bottle into my hands so I could go round collecting the money for him! From there it was a short step to singing with him. "Ooh", he said, "You've got a good voice. You should come to the Jack Hammer folk club in Richmond." So I did, and that's where I played my first gig.

The first time I went there I met a twelve-string guitar player named Johnny Joyce and he and I went out into the car park to work out a blues number that we then went back inside and performed.[15] The audience loved it. Johnny said: "You've got something there, girl, you should build it up." But I was still only sixteen and had no real idea how to move forward, so this thirty- year- old man took me under his wing and together we formed a great little jug band named The Levee Breakers.[16] Mac McGann, the mandolin tipple player, joined us.[17] He could also play six-string guitar and was into ragtime and all sorts of funky blues stuff. A lovely man named Henry became the jug.[18] We called him Henry the Eighth because he was so big and cuddly, and he would literally blow across the mouth of this old stone jug and make a bass sound – it was brilliant! No-one was trying to get into my knickers; we were just musicians making music.

---

[14]**Don Partridge** (b1941) English singer/songwriter and one-man band, known as King of the Buskers. Found fame with his songs 'Rosie' and Blue Eyes'.

[15] **Johnny Joyce** (1933-2004). A legend on the British folk music scene.

[16]**The Levee Breakers.** Not to be confused with the later Led Zeppelin - inspired band of the same name.

[17]**Mac McGann.** Veteran London folk/blues performer.

[18]**Henry the Jug** - real name Michael Bartlett, later member of The Famous Jug Band.

I began to see musicians as more sensitive than actors, whom I was beginning to find a bit pretentious, a bit 'Luvvy darling', and although I continued attending drama school, my heart was turning more and more towards music. Perhaps it was just the times. There was all this new music coming out and you could say everything you wanted in a few lines. I began to find music soothing; it reached me in a way that acting never could, so when I graduated from Corona's, instead of joining the RSC as planned, I chose to go with the music instead, where a glittering career seemed to be beckoning to me. My sister Sandra gave me a lot of encouragement. She was the first one of the family I sang in front of and she was very enthusiastic about it. Every time I went home for the holidays she and I would go off around all the Coventry jazz and folk clubs, where she would proudly introduce me to the audience as her sister when I got up to sing.

I said before that men have always played an important part in my life. Although a lot of them turned out to be shits, I was lucky enough to make some very good male friends at this time. Apart from the jug band boys, I found myself among a terrific bunch of Oxford graduates who let me live for cheap (well, nothing really) in their flat my last year at drama school. Richard Gott was Features Editor of The Guardian, Richard Gilbert worked for BBC Radio 4 and Mike Nash was a social worker with a special interest in Nigeria. We had a great time. It was the era of wine and cheese parties. Loads of interesting people gathered in the flat, people like Tariq Ali, Peggy Duff of the CND, Bertrand Russell's son Conrad - and intelligent conversation flowed with the wine, late into the night.[19]

---

[19]**Tariq Ali** (b1943) Became prominent in the '60s as a left-wing political campaigner. **Peggy Duff** (1910-1981) British political activist. The **Campaign for Nuclear Disarmament** (CND) was founded in 1957 and famously held an annual march from London to Aldermaston to protest the spread of nuclear weapons. Bertrand Russell the philosopher (1872-1970) was its first president and Peggy Duff its first organising secretary.

My flatmates had a wonderful library too, and they gave me unlimited access to it. Richard lent me a book on Woody Guthrie, whom I'd never heard of before. I found that inspiring, the little man against the system, telling it like it is and not being frightened; I was my mother's daughter and I loved it.[20] Dick Gilbert also let me loose among his amazing collection of recordings of American blues artists. That's where I first heard singers like Blind Willie McTell and Big Joe Williams, singers who not only widened my musical horizons but who provided the material for the growing repertoire of The Levee Breakers.[21] I seemed to be going from strength to strength, and then I fell in love.

I remember the first time I saw Bert Jansch.[22] He had that air about him that made you want to mother him, to wash his clothes, cook him a good meal, love him up. I was a silly little girl and I found it irresistible. But he didn't seem to notice me for at least a year until the night The Levee Breakers supported him at a gig in the East End. He came to the front of the crowd and stood there watching me for our entire set, at the end of which he just took me by the hand and dragged me off! That was the start of our relationship. Maybe my voice had summoned him, maybe seeing me on stage had transformed me into 'somebody' in his eyes. I don't know. I only know I thought I was in love with him and he became my first real boyfriend.

I seem to suffer from this romantic streak that turns devils into angels before my eyes. I think it's a trap many girls have fallen into. I wasn't a woman yet. I didn't know anything about making love and turning a man on. I was used to men looking

---

[20]**Woodie Guthrie** (1912-1967) American folk musician known as the 'Dust Bowl Troubadour'. He was a mentor to Bob Dylan and a figurehead of the '60s folk movement.

[21]**Big Joe Williams** (1903-1982) American delta blues guitarist and singer/songwriter. **Blind Willie McTell** (c1898-1959) Influential American blues singer, songwriter and 12 string guitar player.

[22]**Bert Jansch** (b1943) Scottish folk musician. Founding member of the group Pentangle.

at me when I walked into a room, but to all intents and purposes I was an innocent abroad. I put Bert on a pedestal and proceeded to pour all my energy into him. *He* was the important one; *he* had to be kept fit for the stage. I just forgot about myself. I was sacrificing my power for a man but I didn't realise it at the time. What did I get out of it? An illusion of connection, a feeling of adoration just being near him? Maybe deep down I was still trying to make my father love me. I don't remember any great lovemaking. Most of the time we were together Bert sat on the bed writing songs.

That's another thing I've learnt over the years, that many men need a female muse to inspire them. They may not acknowledge her and she may know nothing of the dynamics of what's happening, but it's the woman who sources the music every time. Read Robert Graves' 'The White Goddess' and you'll understand what I'm talking about.[23] Watch the movie 'Made' to understand the exploitation that has always gone on in the music business.[24] But I knew nothing of that. I was virtually a child, alone in London, with an indifferent father behind me and a first love who'd turned out to be gay. What chance did I have? I looked up to Bert as an artiste and I loved him as a man. The songs I inspired appeared on his 1965 album 'It Don't Bother Me'. There's a picture of me on the album sleeve looking like a cone head, hair heaped on the top of my head and the rest cascading round my shoulders, my eyes framed by a heavy fringe. It's a good album, but Bert wasn't a performer.

---

[23]**Robert Graves** (1895-1985) 'The White Goddess - A Historical Grammar of Poetic Myth'. First published by Faber & Faber (1948). In which Graves postulates the idea of a European deity known as The White Goddess of Birth, Love and Death.

[24]**'Made'** (1972) Directed by John Mackenzie. Starring Carol White, Roy Harper and Roy Castle. Tells the story of a single mother and a rock star. Very sad. Carol White (1943-1991) English actress who had leapt to fame playing the lead in 'Cathy Come Home' (1966). Roy Harper (b1941) is an English folk rock singer/songwriter and guitarist. Roy Castle (1932-1994) Popular performer, entertainer and actor also known for his jazz trumpet playing.

He was a brilliant, innovative guitarist and great songwriter, but too moody to shine on stage.

Bert was sharing a flat in Somali Road with John Renbourn, another great guitar player.[25] They were both struggling musicians at this time, living from day to day on whatever they could earn gigging. I spent a lot of time in that flat, returning to my room with the Oxford boys whenever Bert's moodiness indicated that he didn't want me around.

London was at the heart of the 60s' folk music revival and the whole folk music world seemed to converge on Somali Road while I was with Bert. I remember Derroll Adams, sidekick of Ramblin' Jack Elliott, the American banjo player turning up.[26] Dominic Behan, the author of 'The Patriot Game', was a frequent visitor. Alex Campbell came to play.[27] Peter Bellamy, Royston Wood and Heather Wood who made up The Young Tradition also shared the house. They sang classic English folk, unaccompanied. Anne Briggs, a very famous and influential English singer stayed there for a time. Donovan in particular would come round and try to persuade Bert to write songs for him. He was already enjoying chart success as 'England's answer to Bob Dylan', and he fixated on Bert.

In Colin Harper's book about Bert entitled 'Dazzling Stranger' there's a suggestion that I was "putting it about a bit" and that Donovan, Bert and I were having some sort of love triangle. That just wasn't true. I was a kid wrapped up in my first real love affair and although I thought Donovan a nice enough man, he just wasn't for me. I suppose whenever you offer yourself to the public eye you're fair game for all sorts of malicious rumours. It hurts, especially when it's not true. But

---

[25] **John Renbourn** (b1944) British acoustic guitarist and founder member of the group Pentangle.

[26]**Derroll Adams** (1925-2000) American banjo player. Played with Ramblin' Jack Elliott (1927-2001)

[27]**Alex Campbell** (1925-1987) Scottish folk singer and busker.

after all these years it doesn't really matter, it's just good to put the record straight.

The Levee Breakers were going great guns at this point. Mac McGann, Johnny Joyce and myself were the original line-up, with Ralph McTell joining for a few months after Mac decided to quit.[28] Although we hadn't been together very long, we got an invitation to do a recording session at EMI, thanks to a friend of Mac's named Klaus Voormann, who happened to be a close associate of The Beatles. [29]

I knew nothing about the business side of the deal or who signed the contract, but I trusted the band and so we went into the studio and laid down four tracks, included 'Stealin'' and 'Going to Germany', both classic jug band tracks. Somebody told me it was George Martin himself who was in the control room that day, and that this was his little experiment with a group other than The Beatles.[30] Whether that was true or not, the session went well and in 1965 EMI released a track called 'Babe I'm Leaving', a modern jug song penned by Mac. It got played a lot on the BBC but didn't sell that well. Nobody knew where to place it.

The trouble was it was too 'Americana'. Dylan himself had put out a version of 'Stealin'' when he first started. We didn't know this when we recorded it, but we'd added a harmonica to the line up so, without knowing it, we produced a version that was Dylanesque in style.[31] They would have loved it in the States, where artists like Jim

---

[28]**Ralph McTell** (b1944) English guitarist and singer/songwriter who penned 'Streets of London'.

[29]**Klaus Voormann** (b1938) German artist, musician and record producer. Bassist with English band Manfred Mann and also designed the album cover for The Beatles' album 'Revolver'(1966).

[30]**Sir George Martin** (b1926) Producer of all but one of The Beatles' original recordings.

[31]**Bob Dylan** (b1941) Singer/songwriter/poet. Became the voice of the counterculture that was developing in the '60s.

Kweskin[32] and John Sebastian[33] were developing different styles, but over here the folk rock scene was divided into straight rhythm and blues, like John Mayall or electric blues, like Eric Clapton. [34]

I hadn't heard much electric blues yet. I'd met Clapton though, when he came to one of my gigs. He was with Manfred Mann and Tom McGuinness and after I'd sung, this shy young man came up and told me I was great, and it was him.[35] Years later, when he was working with John, we met again. He remembered me from that night and said to John: "What's she doing in your kitchen? She should be out singing." I don't recall John answering that. We spent some good times with Clapton and his lady, Pattie Boyd. I remember once we all went to a fair together and Clapton spent a fortune trying to win a goldfish for Pattie. But that was much later...

I was definitely getting noticed; people would say: "She's young, but she's got a big voice." And then EMI called me and told me they wanted me to ditch the band and record a single called 'The Sins of the Father Fall on the Daughter'. It had been written by P.F. Sloan, who had written 'Eve of Destruction' and their idea was to develop me into an English Cher.[36] It was a

---

[32] **Jim Kweskin** (b1940) Founder of The Jim Kweskin Jug Band that was active in Boston in the 1960s. Played at the famous Newport Folk Festival in 1964.

[33] **John Sebastian** (b 1944) American songwriter and harmonica player. Founder of the group The Lovin' Spoonful.

[34] **John Mayall** (b1933) Pioneering British blues musician and founder of John Mayall and the Bluesbreakers, which fostered many talented young musicians including **Eric Clapton** (b1945), generally recognised as one of the greatest guitarists of all time.

[35] **Manfred Mann** – Founder of British rhythm and blues band that bore his name and flourished from 1962 - 1969. **Tom McGuinness** - guitarist and bass player for Manfred Mann 1964 -1969.

[36] **Cher** (b1946) First rose to prominence as part of singing duo Sonny and Cher and then went on to have a successful solo career as a singer and actress.

great opportunity, and I couldn't wait to tell Bert about it. That was my first big mistake.

Why do we always think our partners are going to be on our side? Lovers aren't parents, and even parents sometimes have their own agendas. But being in love with someone, or even thinking you're in love with them, can turn you into a soppy fool. When I told Bert about the offer he said: "No, no, no. You can't do that. It'll be awful. They'll turn you into something awful." And I believed him.

What I didn't realise was that in reality he just couldn't handle the fact that his girlfriend was being offered a major recording contract when he didn't have one. So I turned down the deal and went with him as he tried to persuade Nat Josephs at Transatlantic Records to record him, using me for a few tracks. But Josephs was having none of it. He told Bert he was a loner, and if he used me I would "stick out like a sore thumb". We carried on doing live gigs together and my voice was getting better all the time, but that was my first shot at the big time and I'd thrown it away for love.

Our relationship didn't last much longer. Bert had been seeing lots of other women behind my back and one night he went off with someone and that was the end of it. I was devastated and hid myself away for six months. I didn't waste that time though. I spent it improving my guitar playing. Johnny Joyce from The Levee Breakers had shown me how to play my first chord, but it was Bert who taught me how to play well. I may have had a broken heart again, but at least I'd learned how to play a mean guitar.

CHAPTER 3

London – Monterey – London 1966-1967

Time truly is the great healer. Eventually I began to visit old haunts again - coffee and a sandwich and good folk music - it all helped to mend that broken heart. It was at one such club where I had done some gigs that I first met Paul Simon and Art Garfunkel in 1965.[37] They had seen me perform and came over to congratulate me. "You were great" were the words, I think. "Yeah", I responded cheekily, and we got on famously.

They were a couple of New Yorkers who stuck out like sore thumbs on the London folk scene; where the Brits were hairy and dirty, Paul and Artie were pristine clean and neat in their cream-coloured mackintoshes. They could've been gay, they were so well turned out. They'd already had a massive hit in the States as Tom and Jerry with a bubblegum number called 'Hey schoolgirl in the second row' but now when I ran into Paul again, he was alone and really excited to tell me that he'd just heard that their new single was racing up the American charts. They'd put an electric backing on one of their songs and 'Sound of Silence' was on its way to becoming an all-time classic.

By now, I had graduated from drama school. I was offered the job with the Royal Shakespeare Company, but I had already found myself an agent and signed with Decca as the first artist on their new Deram Label, which started up in 1966,

---

[37]**Simon & Garfunkel.** The duo rose to fame in the '60s as one of the seminal sounds of their generation.

so being Vanessa Redgrave's handmaid for the next few years held no attraction for me.[38] I was itching to do stuff and wanted to go with the music - no-one could talk me out of it. The agent was Denny Cordell, one of a new breed of young music agents who sprang up in the '60s. He was in his early twenties with the business head of a thirty something. He was well-educated and hip and had his finger on the pulse. I was the lamb to the slaughter, if I'd only realised it.

The second signing for Deram was Cat Stevens, later known as Yusuf Islam.[39] I remember we were both the guests of honour at the launch party of the new label and we coincidentally turned up dressed all in white – me in satin and lace and him in a white suit and shirt. We escaped from the party very early because it was too boring; it was full of old bald-heads from the music industry and a smattering of DJs getting very pissed on the free booze.

Cat took me up to his parents' flat above their fish and chip shop at Cambridge Circus, right in the heart of theatre land. We sat in the lounge and his parents brought us coffee. We began playing our music to each other and then he suddenly planted a big kiss on me. I didn't take it any further because I didn't fancy him but I always remember his saying: "You'll never make it because you're too pure", which was a sort of backhanded compliment I suppose, but proved to be somewhat prophetic too.

If you want to be out there and succeed in the music business, you have to stage manage your life. You have to get people's attention, knock on doors, do people's heads in, drive them mad. It's as if you have to announce: "Hi, I'm on coke. I'm going fifty miles an hour and where's the party? Let's talk about me. Let's have a jam, let's write something." It has to be

---

[38]**Vanessa Redgrave** (b 1937) Oscar-winning actress and member of the famous Redgrave acting dynasty.

[39]**Cat Stevens/Yusuf Islam** (b1948) British singer/songwriter. He changed his name in 1978 after converting to Islam.

that full on and it can be very short lived because it's so easy to burn yourself out. If you're not that sort of person, you can easily get elbowed out of the way by someone else's scramble to the top.

Denny Cordell was the first big man to come along and say: "I'm gonna make you a star". He began grooming me for stardom, dressing me in the most exquisite gear from the trendiest boutiques in Sloane Square and South Kensington, all velvet and lace, turning me into a Beardsley type 'lady', teaching me how to drink brandy 'properly' and not blow smoke through my nose.[40] All the time he was telling me how much money he had got from the record label for me. He assured me I didn't need to sign anything. He said he'd tell me when I had to because I would need to get my mother to sign on my behalf since I was still a teenager. But I never saw any of the money – looking back I can't believe how naive and trusting I was. I'm not saying anything illegal was happening, but in the music business you are swimming with the sharks and it's easy to get bitten.

There were a lot of men like him around at that time, men who rose to fortune on the backs of their artists and managed to buy themselves Porsches while the poor singer was living on bread and Marmite.[41] I instinctively knew there was something creepy about Cordell because he was always trying to get into my knickers but I was only eighteen and full of mystical dreams. Mind you, that was when I began to learn how nasty men can be when you turn them down. I had thought him such a great guy. I loved his musical taste and he turned me on to a lot of great musicians but I felt he had no real respect for me, like I was just a silly girl to be

---

[40]**Aubrey Beardsley** (1872-1898) English Art Nouveau author and illustrator. Contemporary of Oscar Wilde's.

[41]Leonard Cohen, David Bowie, Steve Marriott and the group Bad Finger are just some who suffered from shady management at some point in their careers.

taken advantage of. He always managed to make me feel like the serving wench who had been summoned up to the master's room!

I had to be seen in all the right places with all the right people and I certainly went to a lot of interesting parties. I remember one in Islington at the home of a woman named Sandra Harries.[42] She and her partner were an American couple who had settled in London as refugees from the nightmare of McCarthyism. It was in the 1950s, during the early days of the Cold War, that Republican Senator Joseph McCarthy launched a witchhunt in the US against anyone suspected of being a Communist. America at that time was no place to be for anyone with the slightest Socialist leanings; the mere accusation of left-wing sympathies past or present was enough to get you blacklisted and hounded out of your profession; people were pressurised to denounce friends and colleagues to save their own skins. It was a horrible period in American history. It seems a long time ago now, but in 1967 it was still a recent event. The purges affected people from all walks of life, but especially the performing arts. No-one was immune and those who could leave got out of the country to work elsewhere, including this deliciously bohemian Jewish couple who had been heavily involved in left-wing theatre in New York.

I was at the party with another American, an actor named Weston Gavin, who was doing stand-up comedy at Les Cousins, Greek Street at the time and I got to meet Tommy Smothers, of Smothers Brothers fame[43], and Peter Cook, who spent the evening getting more and more pissed and slagging

---

[42]**Sandra Harris.** Best known in the UK as the co-writer, with jazz singer Blossom Dearie, of '60s hit 'Sweet Georgie Fame'.

[43]**The Smothers Brothers.** Singing comedy duo whose TV show 'The Smothers Brothers Comedy Hour' became one of the most controversial TV shows of the Vietnam War period and was cancelled by CBS in 1969 for its anti-establishment bias.

off everyone there.[44] Luckily he seemed to take a shine to me. "Don't change," he slurred at me, "Be your lovely innocent self". I was eighteen and I thought that was awfully sweet.

The buzz at the party was that Barbra Streisand was going to put in an appearance.[45] When the great lady did arrive, she came accompanied by her entourage, which consisted of two people - her hairdresser and her black maid.

Now an interesting thing about Streisand is that she apparently never performs where she can see the audience looking at her, so she wasn't someone who was going to burst into song at a party. People had been asking me to play all evening and now Tommy Smothers came over and urged me again to start performing. It seemed a good time, so I started strumming and singing while Ms Streisand was doing the party round. She didn't stay long, but before she swept out, she came over to me and said: "I see I have competition," and gave me a genuinely warm smile. I felt like she'd recognised a sister in me and that made me feel very good.

All this time there were press releases penned by Cordell himself to keep me in the public eye in the lead up to my first recording for Deram. The label arranged a fabulous line up of musicians to back me on that first single. I had Jimmy Page on guitar, John Paul Jones on bass, Andy White on drums and Nicky Hopkins on piano.[46] Unfortunately, the song they chose for me was Randy Newman's 'Happy New Year' which was

---

[44]**Peter Cook** (1937-1995) British writer, satirist and comedian. Enjoyed a successful partnership with Dudley Moore (1935-2002), who himself found hollywood fame as an actor.

[45]**Barbra Streisand** (b1942) Oscar-winning American singer, actress and film-maker.

[46] **Jimmy Page** (b1944) English rock guitarist and founder of Led Zeppelin. **John Paul Jones** (b1946) Bass and keyboard player for Led Zeppelin. **Andy White** (b1930) Scottish session drummer who played on the first Beatles' single 'Love Me Do'. **Nicky Hopkins** (1944-1994) Legendary session keyboard player.

too dark for the time and didn't catch on. But the company Cordell had created, seemingly on my advance, flourished. He signed Joe Cocker, Denny Lane, Procul Harum, The Move – he was churning out hits every week.[47] He just knew the sound of the day and he was determined to make money. He did.

I ignored my instincts about him because I was desperate to be a success so I could help my mother get out of her hard times and Denny would promise me the moon, saying: "You'll be able to buy ribbons for your mother every day" but again, I never saw any of the money I was supposedly earning.

He had no real idea of poverty. They were all like that, the Chelsea boys, as I called them. Men who came from upper-class families, and all knew each other. They were experimenting with acid, indulging in coke and heroin. They were ruthless public school boys who seemed above the law. As Dylan wrote: 'Steal a little and they throw you in jail, steal a lot and they make you king.' They looked cool in their velvet suits, suede boots and long flowing hair and they called themselves managers and producers but they were no humanitarians, they didn't care who they exploited to achieve their ride on the gravy train. They were greedy bastards; scavengers, every one of them.

Artists always have been and always will be vulnerable financially because most of us haven't the first idea about business. We want to make our music, that's where our talent lies, not on balance sheets. It's a rare artist who can function successfully in both worlds. And you have to trust people, especially when you're young and wanting to get a foot in the door. Have things changed today? One can hope there is more protection for the up and coming, but the sad truth is that wherever money exists, so too do unscrupulous piranhas.

It was in June 1967 that I was invited to perform at the Monterey Pop Festival, as a guest of Simon and Garfunkel. Paul and I had grown close. It was both a romance and a really

---

[47] Joe Cocker, Denny Lane, Procul Harum, The Move - all some of the biggest-selling UK recording artists of the '60s.

good friendship, and the best possible introduction to the States. But my mother had become very ill, suffering from cancer of the stomach, and I wasn't sure about flying off while she was so sick; I was devastated and couldn't think of anything but her well-being. But being her, she insisted that I went, especially when I told her I would be going to Monterey. I think she had romantic notions about the place from the Steinbeck books she'd read as a girl and she was really happy to think of her daughter going there.[48] So I put aside my misgivings and took her at her word.

In America Paul and Artie took me all over the country to their gigs. We went to every major college campus in the country where they played massive indoor basketball arenas. They loved playing to college kids, they thought the next President of the United States might be sitting in one of those audiences and they had a chance to get through to him with their music. They really believed they could somehow turn on a nation politically with songs like 'The Sound of Silence', and perhaps they did.

Some of the time we'd just hang out together, playing music, going to theatres or just walking the streets of New York, which they knew inside out. They were both great walkers and we would spend hours exploring places like The Village. They were such good fun to be with, always creating a little magic wherever they went. In the streets people would call out 'Hey, Simon, hey, Garfunkel' and they'd wave back. There were no paparazzi in those days sticking their cameras up your nose at every turn, so their celebrity didn't stop them from having fun like ordinary people.

Paul and Artie were both Jewish but they were so different from British Jews. They were Americans first, Jews second, totally assimilated and liberated. I loved their company and

---

[48] John Steinbeck (1902-1968) American Nobel Prize-winning author, famous for his books set in California and during the Great Depression of the 1930s.

Paul and I had slipped into a really intimate relationship. He was the first man I'd been to bed with since Bert. I thought he was a warm, huggable man and very, very funny, although, like everyone else, he had his moody days when he just went off on his own. He did offer to marry me at one point to give me a green card, but I didn't think that was very romantic, and anyway, I was far too young to think about marriage. More to the point, I felt I needed emotional, not financial security. By the time we got to Monterey, he had begun to go a bit weird on me.

California 1967, the Summer of Love.[49] Things were beginning to get what I can only call 'fluffy'. People began talking about New Age things such as 'channelling', receiving messages from a teaching spirit. I had never heard about crystals, or ley lines, stuff like that, it was all above my head. I remember there were stories of mysterious goings on in a place called Bohemian Grove in Monte Rio but it was years before word really began to get out about it. Apparently, it is a private campsite owned by an exclusive San Francisco-based men's arts club which plays host for three weeks a year to some of the most powerful men in the worlds of politics and business. What goes on there is kept strictly secret but rumour has it that they perform rituals dressed in black, including one where they burn an effigy of an owl to represent 'killing care' for another year. It wasn't until much later that conspiracy theorists identified them as the Illuminati, the ultimate powers-that-be who dominate our world from behind the scenes. In later years I would read books written about them, but back then, I was too inexperienced to really know anything of what was going on. I kept my mouth shut and my ears open.

Just before the Festival started, while we were still in Los Angeles, David Crosby took me up to his place in Laurel

---

[49]**The Summer of Love** 1967. When San Francisco became the centre of the hippie revolution.

Canyon to do some recording for him.[50] He was still playing with The Byrds then, before Crosby, Stills, Nash and Young got together, and I had met him when Paul and I had sat in on one of their recording sessions. That was where I experienced my first earthquake, fortunately only a minor tremor, but scary enough. You couldn't help but like David. He was a happy, friendly soul and his little house was delightful, full of top drawer hippy stuff with tasteful rugs and cushions scattered everywhere. He made me feel very relaxed and I laid down a few tracks for him but I don't remember much about that session, because he lit up some very good weed as soon as we got there and after we'd smoked that, the rest was a blur.

I do remember this stunningly handsome young man turning up who was introduced to me as Peter. When it was time to get back down to the Beverly Wilshire Hotel where Paul and I were staying, this Peter offered to drive me back in his Range Rover. I was happy to accept his offer and off we went. He asked me lots of questions about myself as we were driving and we got back in one piece OK, although he drove frighteningly close to the mountain edge all the way down. As we arrived at the hotel, he asked me if I was with anybody and I told him Paul Simon. That was the end of that. It was Paul himself who later told me my chauffeur was Peter Fonda. What a missed opportunity! A couple of years' later when I went to see 'Easy Rider', I could swear he was wearing the same leather trousers he'd had on that day in Laurel Canyon. Perhaps he was always in character.[51]

Paul was somewhat distant with me at Monterey. He'd decided he wanted to be free there and he sent me off to amuse

---

[50]David Crosby (b1944) Influential American guitarist and singer.

[51]Peter Fonda (b1940). American actor and film-maker, son of Henry, brother of Jane, father of Bridget and Justin. 'Easy Rider' (1969) was a landmark American road movie charting the experiences of two motorbike-riding drug dealers.

myself so I had plenty of time on my own to hang out with some of the wonderful, talented people gathered there.

The great Otis Redding I remember as what I can only describe as a 'grown man', so well-groomed and smartly dressed.[52] I had a friendly date with handsome Scott McKenzie who was enjoying a huge hit with 'If You're Going to San Francisco'. Artie carried me off one afternoon to see the new Dylan movie 'Don't Look Back', which had just opened. At one point Janis Joplin slapped me on the back like a bloke and growled, "Write your own stuff, huh?"[53] Then she offered to share her bottle of Southern Comfort with me, but I had to decline; I've never been a big drinker. I even had an obsessive fan in the shape of Phil Ochs, another singer/songwriter, well-known in the States for his 'protest songs'. He followed me around constantly and although I'd heard *of* him, I'd never met him before, so I didn't recognise him and supposed he was just some weird guy stalking me, even though he was cute. I heard later that he developed bi-polar disorder and committed suicide in 1976. Another beautiful young man who died before his time.

I got to sing on the first night of the festival. I played two songs acoustic, 'Sweet Honesty' and 'Sweet Joy', and then a little-known Donovan song 'Picking out the Sunshine' backed by the house band who had played for Lou Rawls, the act before me.[54] We were massively under-rehearsed, as there was only time for us to run through the song once; it didn't really get into any kind of a groove. But I did it and it felt good.

Although California had already experienced the Grateful Dead's psychedelic 'Acid Test' parties, Monterey was the first

---

[52]**Otis Redding** (1941-1967) The 'King of Soul', who tragically died young in a plane crash.

[53]**Janis Joplin** (1943-1970) Pioneering female pioneer rocker who died from a probably accidental heroin overdose.

[54]**Lou Rawls** (1933-2006) American soul, blues and jazz singer.

of the great rock festivals.[55] It set the standard for all the rest, including Woodstock two years later. The line-up included the Dead themselves as well as Jimi Hendrix and The Who, both in their first big American gigs. Janis Joplin and Otis Redding were playing their first major public performances there while Jefferson Airplane, The Mamas and the Papas, Canned Heat, Country Joe and the Fish all appeared on the bill. Somewhere around 200,000 people came to share the music, with between 55,000 and 90,000 there on the last night alone. I remember the smell of incense on the afternoon Ravi Shankar played and how the Indian *ragas* winged their way round the arena. How spiritual it felt, how amazing that so many aware people were there together in one place. It was so different from my parents' generation when all they'd known was war.[56]

One of the oddest memories I have of Monterey is of attending a weird party in Hugh Hefner's room in the Highlands Inn motel, though not as a Playmate, I hasten to add.[57] The motel had been taken over for the Festival and all the musicians were staying there. It was decorated with fake tartans and cosy fire places, an American idea of Scotland. There were a lot of people there this particular evening and Hefner was sitting next to Tommy Smothers, who I'd met in London. I could see they were both in a very playful mood, sharing lots of private jokes with each other. Then Paul Simon arrived with a young woman in tow who had just recently been delivered of a baby. She started breast-feeding in the middle of the party and when she and Paul left the room, Hefner turned to Tommy and said: "Did you see that?" "Yes. Disgusting." Hefner agreed and I never forgot the hypocrisy. Here was a man obsessed with tits,

---

[55]**Grateful Dead.** Legendary American rock band formed in the San Francisco Bay area in 1965.

[56]All the performers mentioned became major recording stars of the '60s and '70s.

[57]**Hugh Hefner** (b1926) American magazine publisher and founder of Playboy.

the founder of the Playboy empire, who found breast-feeding a child repulsive. I became Mouse again and I listened.

The next day was the last of the festival and Hefner asked me to take a large candle as a gift to Lou Adler, the music producer of the Mamas and the Papas and one of the producers of the festival.[58] I was intrigued by this and couldn't resist glancing at the attached card. It read something like: 'I hope this is big enough for you'. I thought he was taking the piss out of the festival and here was I, carrying this gift like a torch! When Adler read the note, he had a weird look on his face. I thought they were putting it down, peace and love and all that as crap. Everything has its darker side, even charity gigs in the Summer of Love.

That last night, Jimi Hendrix performed and, as he set his guitar ablaze at the end of 'Wild Thing', I was convinced I could see my mother's face coming towards me out of the flames, as if it were a funeral pyre. In that instant I knew instinctively that she had died. It was a chilling experience and it affected me deeply; I began to go a bit strange after that. Remember, this was the '60s, there were no mobile phones to hand, no quick way to phone home from the middle of a field. And I didn't want to know for sure. Not then. Not yet. I couldn't face the reality. I couldn't bear it.[59]

I spent four months in the States altogether. It seemed like a lifetime because I was flying everywhere, going to a different city every day but after Monterey, Paul became more and more distant with me. I think he was used to women who were after him because of who he was, but I was a fellow musician, not a giggling groupie. I used to enjoy jamming with him and Artie. It's my voice and my line you hear on 'Fakin' It', but you won't find my name on the album. There would be similar incidents over the years, especially after I married John but musicians inspire each other, that's what we do. I remember one day I was

---

[58] **Lou Adler** (b1933) American record producer, manager and director.

[59] **Jimi Hendrix** (1942-1970) Arguably the greatest electric guitarist of all.

playing around with a song about the ocean when Paul came into the room. Shortly after, he wrote 'Bridge Over Troubled Water.' Did I inspire him? I hope so. It's a good feeling to be part of something creative.

We were all supposed to go back to New York after Monterey, but I wanted to stay in California and spend some time in San Francisco. When I told Paul this, he just threw my return ticket at me, said "Bye!" and walked out, slamming the door. Someone had found me a room in the house where the Steve Miller Band were living and I moved in there. Artie and his girlfriend stayed with me the first night because they were worried about me but he had to go back to New York too, so he gave me some money and told me to look after myself. It was an ironic place to be for someone who was on the edge of some sort of breakdown; The Grateful Dead were living in the house next door.

It was that summer that the Haight-Ashbury area of San Francisco saw the flowering of the hippy movement and the spread of consciousness-changing psychedelic substances, mainly in the form of LSD[60]. The Grateful Dead were at the heart of this movement and their soundman Owsley Stanley (aka The Bear) was the first underground cook/alchemist/chemist, call him what you will, to produce large quantities of the drug and hand it out to the people, often for nothing; everyone in that house seemed to be doing a lot of acid a lot of the time.

Owsley was a character. A small man, going bald but with strands of very thin wispy hair, he'd been born in Australia and was a good ten years older than everyone else around. He seemed to know everybody who was anybody on the A-list of celebrities and is credited with having produced and distributed anything from one million to five million hits of acid. I think the gods of good sense must have been keeping an eye on me at the time. I was offered some LSD but didn't feel it was the right

---

[60]**LSD** - Lysergic Acid Diethylamide.

time or place to start experimenting with that. I just wasn't in the right frame of mind. I dread to think what would have happened if I had taken any then. I might have floated off into some hippy nightmare and never been heard of again.

I spent more time with The Steve Miller boys.[61] They were backing Chuck Berry while he was supporting Jimi Hendrix at the Fillmore Auditorium in San Francisco. I knew Mitch Mitchell, Hendrix' drummer, as we'd been at the Corona Stage School together, so I spent a whole week watching these great musicians perform and hanging out backstage with them in the dressing rooms. I remember Chuck Berry as a terrific showman who intertwined his songs with poetry, while watching Hendrix was always a wonderful experience; the man shone on stage. In the dressing rooms, he was forever surrounded by a bevy of glamorous women although he was always very shy with me.

I still hadn't confirmed whether my mother was dead but I had the feeling that somebody knew something. Perhaps Paul knew but didn't tell me because he thought that I would freak. Anyway, there wasn't a man there who could say: "She needs a good hug". So I hung out in the Miller house, just helping out and doing a bit of cooking and avoiding going home. It was only Tim Davis, their beautiful Afro-American drummer, who eventually saw there was something going wrong with me and who looked after me for a couple of weeks, not in a lecherous way, but as a human being.[62]

Tim was a tall, virile figure of a man who liked to wear a cowboy hat that made him even more imposing and I'll never forget the day we went into a hamburger joint and the waitress took one look at this stunning black man and rudely demanded that he take off the hat. He politely refused and we left the place but I think that was the first time I realised just how difficult life could be for a black man in America.

---

[61]**Steve Miller Band.** Rock Band formed in San Francisco in 1967.

[62]**Tim Davis** (1943-1988) Co-founder of The Steve Miller Band

I finally got myself onto a plane back to New York. Paul phoned me and suggested I wait there for him until he got back from a trip to Canada as there was nothing really waiting for me at home. But I knew he wasn't the right man for me and I knew I had to find out what was happening at home sooner or later, so I eventually flew back to London where I learned my mother had died the very night I had sensed it at Monterey. My heart almost stopped with fright when they told me.

CHAPTER 4

London – Woodstock – London 1967-1969

I didn't go straight up to Coventry. I didn't even want to phone the family at first. Aside from losing my mother, I didn't know what was happening to my career. It was as if my life were crumbling around me. I finally went back to a lot of "Where were you?" and "How could you not be there?" from the family. There were no hugs, no family grieving together; I had been gone for too long. There had been no big funeral, just a small cremation attended by a few friends. To tell the truth, part of me was relieved that I hadn't had to see her in all that pain. But that was a selfish, childish reaction. I tried to console myself with the thought that it had given her pleasure to know I was in Monterey. But they told me she had hung on, asking for me and, of course, the horror of my not being there affected me deeply.

Denny Cordell was still my manager but he was trying to offload me onto someone else. He now had a massive hit with Procul Harum and 'A Whiter Shade of Pale'; he'd lost interest in me. I recorded a version of 'Museum', a Donovan song, but it was put out with a Georgie Fame and the Blue Flames' instrumental entitled 'A Quick One for Sanity' on the B side; Cordell's wife's name was on the label as producer.[63]

---

[63]**Georgie Fame** (b1943) British rhythm 'n' blues and jazz keyboard player and singer.

I refused to promote it because I thought that was tacky and they said I'd broken my contract. I was still hopeless with business and now my mum was gone, there was no-one to help me sort things out. Paul had been right, I had come back to nothing, no mother and no career. I just could not take on board the reality of her death. I was haunted by the feeling that I'd been selfish in not coming home sooner, even though there was nothing I could have done to stop her dying. I began spiralling out of control. I was in such a poor state emotionally that it wasn't surprising I got pregnant.

Although the father didn't want to take responsibility for the situation, I decided that I was going to have this child and keep it; I was determined I could cope. Looking back, I think I was trying to cop out for a while. I'd been to America and seen it and it was scary. My career here was in the doldrums and I'd lost my comforting, sensible, loving mother; I needed something to love. My first-born son would fill that hole. And two months before his birth, I landed a deal with Joe Boyd's company Witchseason Productions Ltd, producers of Warlock Music Ltd. Joe himself was a very tall, beautiful-looking young American with blue eyes and good cheekbones who had based himself in England. Here he discovered Nick Drake, The Incredible String Band and Fairport Convention.[64] I'd done a tape for Joe and he told me to go off and have my baby and they'd look after me. Life began to look up.

It wasn't easy finding accommodation for a single mother and baby in those days. Thanks to Joe and his friend Caroline Coon, co-founder of Release, who worked really hard on my behalf, I got a room in a home for unmarried mothers.[65] It was

---

[64]**Nick Drake** (1948-1974) English singer/songwriter who only found fame posthumously. **The Incredible String Band** - pioneering psychedelic Scottish folk band formed in 1965. They split up in 1974 but reformed 1999-2006. **Fairport Convention**–Influential English electric folk rock band formed in 1967.

[65]**Release**–UK agency set up in 1967 to provide legal advice and representation for young people arrested for drug possession.

clean, each woman had a room to herself with a cooker in it and we all shared bathrooms. It was ideal. Joe kept me on a retainer of £15 a week, not bad money in the '60s, but not a fortune, and out of that I had to pay for everything - rent, nappies, laundry. After six months it went up to £20 when someone must have mentioned that I was looking very thin. I gradually started doing bits of recording for Witchseason and it was at this time that I first met Nick Drake.

I was in the studio recording one day when this shy young man came in. He was tall like Joe Boyd but hunched over because he never had any confidence. I thought he was a bit of an odd character until I heard his music and realised how good it was. Joe would encourage us to hang out together. He'd take us to art galleries and concerts and we'd often play cards together. Nick would occasionally say something witty, but very rarely. He was very interested in hearing me talk about Bert and John Renbourn but he was never the life and soul of the party. All of us involved in the label got used to his being around and I grew to love him like a brother, in a protective kind of way. So I had a recording deal and good friends around and a beautiful baby boy to take care of. Joe was even planning to take me over to the States to produce and record my first album for Warner Brothers; life was getting better and better...

Is it Sod's Law that just when things start to go right, the gods send a cosmic spanner that lands smack bang in the heart of the works? In spite of all the good things that were happening in my life, in spite of the fact that I was now a mother myself, inside I was still the little girl cowering at the sound of her father's brutality, a child who had lost her mother and was looking for love. That's who I see when I look back down the corridor of years. That's who met John Martyn one fateful September night in 1968 at the Chelsea College of Art Folk Club, and that's who was knocked sideways by this angelic-looking hippy child with bare feet and flowing hair who, even then, played a beautiful guitar.

I admit again that men have always played an important part in my life, and I've trusted them when I shouldn't have done. I've no doubt a Freudian psychologist would put it all down to my relationship, or non-relationship, with my father. Whatever it was that made me vulnerable to 'bad boys', when I met this beautiful-looking boy musician I was completely bowled over by him.

I had been taken to the gig by a mutual friend, the folk singer Jackson C. Frank.[66] He told me to bring my guitar along so I could do a song and also meet this Scottish guy, Johnny. The boy I met was enchanting, ethereal, so unlike the man I would later leave. He was brilliant even then, people wanted to see this energetic young man with the gift of the gab and the eyes of a Botticelli angel. I sang, then he sang. Years later John described our meeting to a magazine, "I saw this face with big eyes and big hooter and big tits and I just had to look twice!" When we went out on our first proper date together we went to a trendy bistro in Chelsea where the menu was in French. He really surprised me by talking to the waiter in fluent French. He told me he'd spent a summer across the Channel and managed to pick up the language there. The girl from Coventry was duly impressed. My son wasn't yet a year old and my sister was delighted to take charge of him for a couple of weeks, so John and I could have some quality time together getting to know each other; we went everywhere together in those early days; we were inseparable.

John had been born in Surrey in 1948 but his parents divorced when he was five and his mother left him for long periods to be brought up by his Granny in Glasgow. He had been an only child until his mother remarried when he was in his late teens and gave him a half-brother and –sister but until

---

[66] Jackson C. Frank(1943-1999) was an American who had been terribly burned in a fire at his school when he was 11; at 21 he came to England as a singer/songwriter on the compensation money. In spite of his early success, by 1966 he had begun to suffer from depression and mental problems which plagued him for the rest of his life.

then he'd had his grandmother's sole attention. I was too inexperienced to realise what damage this might have done to him, especially as he didn't display any signs of disturbance in those first, magical days. More to the point, I knew nothing of the bad reputation he had in Glasgow; he had a background of violence and a criminal record that he didn't mention to me. I didn't even realise that his English accent was assumed, the result of years of visiting his mother who lived in London. Later I would hear too often his natural Glasgow growl. At the time, it was one of those intense meetings that seem like magic. We couldn't bear to be out of each other's company for days on end.

What I did eventually learn the hard way was that Granny-reared boys are the worst of all to live with. If she's alive, Granny's still making them pancakes every day, scrubbing everything, dear, and 'have you got clean undies'? Always trying to make up for the fact the mother's not there. So any woman is expected to be in the background, doing women's work with grace – just like Granny. I did meet John's grand-mother when she was about 80. She was a great old woman who could still thrash out a mean ragtime on the piano and I liked her very much. But in those early days there was no hint of the darkness to come and so I made the second biggest mistake of my career.

I told Joe Boyd I'd met this Glaswegian guitarist and wanted to work with him. Joe may have known something of John's reputation, although he didn't mention it. "Bad scene, David McGeachy (John's real name)", was all he said. I think he may have been trying to warn me off, but I was enchanted and in love.

If John's image was an act, it seemed real to me. Some people who knew him, like Linda Thompson, thought him a show off but I thought he was amazing.[67] The music we were working on together was very special and Joe was really excited by it.

---

[67]**Linda Thompson** (b1947) Folk singer and ex-wife of guitarist Richard Thompson (b1949).

It was when he suggested that we go to the States to record that John asked me to marry him, and we did the deed at Hampstead Registry Office in April 1969. Joe Boyd came bringing Nick Drake with him and John's mother turned up as well. We all went back to our little flat in Hampstead where John had made a massive chicken curry. Everyone sat around rolling joints and Joe saved the day by getting hold of some bottles of champagne and glasses to drink it from. John's mother thought our wedding party was 'like a strange play' and 'so Bohemian'! I think I was always the 'older woman' (by 18 months) in his family's eyes.

Our first stop in America was the famous Chelsea Hotel in New York and then we went up to Woodstock where they'd rented a house for us both for three months while we were rehearsing the songs for what was originally meant to be my solo album, produced by Joe Boyd. Woodstock is an up-market artists' colony set in beautiful countryside. Even Dylan had a house there. We arrived in August just before the Woodstock Festival got going, and though that was taking place about fifty miles away in a place called Bethel, Woodstock itself was full of people who thought they were going to hang out in Bob Dylan's back garden. The story goes that he declined to perform at the festival because he was so disgusted by all the hippies gathering round his house...

You could feel the festival vibe everywhere and there was also a buzz about us, the British couple, so we were meeting a lot of fine musicians, including friends of Dylan's, such as Happy and Artie Traum, two well-known bluegrass musicians.[68] Another was our bass player, Harvey Brooks, who later also played on Miles Davis' classic album 'Bitches Brew.'[69] He was a lovely Jewish man who liked the fact there was smoked salmon in our fridge when he came to rehearse, although he always insisted on bringing his own bagels.

---

[68]Happy (b1938) and **Artie Traum** (1943-2008)

[69]**Harvey Brooks** (b1944) Folk rock's first prominent bass guitarist.

We were staying in an attractive little house with a porch where we could sit out nights, soaking in the smell of the pines and watching the fireflies dance, a whole new experience for me. There were woods all around us and strange crickets that popped into your house if you left the door open. There were also snakes that came slithering out of the trees but fortunately, we never met any of those.

Neither John nor I could drive, which is a definite handicap in The States, where practically everyone drives from the age of 16 onwards, but our neighbours were really kind and offered to take us in their car on hot days up to Palenville, a hamlet buried away in upstate New York in the Catskill Mountains. It was stunningly beautiful there. There was a fast-flowing stream running downhill and John used to love riding down in an inflated inner tyre. He would arrive at the bottom battered and bruised, but that never put him off. He was adventurous like that, always risking deep or fast flowing water when he was fishing or just because he wanted to cross to the other side. I, on the other hand, didn't even like swimming, but I would sit and play with the baby, relishing this lush corner of America which we always seemed to have to ourselves. I would daydream about living in this wilderness, but in truth, with a small child I was much more comfortable in Woodstock, which at least had a super-market in the village.

On our way to or from this paradise, we would stop at this little out of the way hamburger joint, run by a big, broad Italian whose name we never found out. John was convinced he was a member of the Mafia. We would fanta-sise that the Cosa Nostra held their secret meetings in the back room, which was all set out with rows of chairs. What really fed our fantasy was when the host turned the juke box on. He had a song on it he'd once recorded entitled: 'You thought you was a wise guy, but you really was a chump' and he'd sing along as it was playing. He was friends with this elderly couple who were childless and who fell in love with my little boy. They obviously thought we were a pair of dippy hippies who couldn't afford to look after a baby because offered to buy him from us for $35,000, an offer we graciously declined.

Although the album was originally supposed to be my solo album, John's contribution got bigger and bigger and the music we were making together was so good it seemed the right direction to go in. We did our rehearsing for the album in the house in Woodstock. There was an organ there, which Paul Harris, our musical director would play and Levon Helm of The Band came over to play drums on a couple of tracks.[70] John and I were already being seen as a duo so it didn't take long for us to be invited to take part in a charity gig to be played in Woodstock Playhouse on the weekend of July 4th. It was in aid of Pete Seeger's Clearwater Project which was committed to cleaning up the Hudson River, and a lot of first-rate folk and blues musicians would be playing on the night. I can't tell you the names of all the musicians who performed because I was so bedazzled by the line-up that my memory is just a kaleidoscope of great music. Sadly the old Playhouse burnt down in 1988, a victim of arson.

It was a strange night, the night of the concert. It felt as if there were an electric storm brewing. For some reason known only to him, John decided he didn't want me to do much singing so he performed five or six numbers before he called me on stage. I did one song, a 'Mr Jelly Roll Baker' blues and that was it. I walked off to thunderous applause and wolf whistles and John finished what was supposed to be our spot on his own.

At the end of the evening, everyone gathered in the foyer and somehow, John and I got split up. I was wondering what to do, when I see this character walking through the door. It was Bob Dylan. He was tiny, gazelle-like, wearing a black

---

[70]**Levon Helm** (b1940) American rock musician, best known as the drummer for The Band, which flourished 1967- 1976 and reformed 1983-1999.

frock coat, and a white shirt. He looked like a *yeshiva* boy in his gold spectacles, a student of the Talmud.[71] I have to explain here that I had been an ardent devotee of Dylan's ever since I was fifteen and my mother called me into the front room to see this interesting-looking young man appearing on TV in a now-lost BBC play called 'Madhouse on Castle Street'. It was the first time anyone here heard 'Blowing in the Wind' and I was smitten. So here was my idol standing talking to my husband. And then I saw that the man himself was looking at me.

He began walking towards me. I was racking my brains to think what I could say to this man whose music had so influenced my life. "I'm really pleased to meet you", he said. "Oh, you can't possibly know what it's like to meet you", I gurgled back and he laughed and took my hand, pulling me towards him so I could kiss him on his cheek. I thought for a moment he was staring at my breasts, but I quickly realised he had his eye fixed on this horned pendant hanging round my neck, a present from John.

I had no idea of its significance but these men all knew more than I did then about mythology and the muse, and how some men use women to inspire them. I felt Dylan was looking into my soul, that we had known each other in another life. It sounds crazy, but there was this instant empathy. Then he noticed that one of my moccasins was unlaced and for a moment I had this intense feeling that he was going to kneel down and lace it up for me. But at that moment John marched over and pulled us apart. Even worse, he pushed me. I heard Dylan say something like "Don't hurt her, man, she's only saying hello to me," and then John snarled at me to get into the car.

As we left, I turned to look out of the back window of the van we were riding in. There was Dylan standing alone with his collar turned up, watching us drive away. What had happened?

---

[71]*Yeshiva* **boy** (Hebrew) A religious student of any school that teaches Torah, Mishnah and Talmud. Traditionally associated with Orthodox Judaism.

I was mortified with embarrassment. But it was when we got back to the house that trouble really started and a side of John came out that I'd never seen before. He went berserk.

He started shouting and throwing things at me, including a fork that hit me under the eye. I thought he'd gone mad, that he was a nutter. It was terrifying. I'd had no idea that he was capable of this sort of violence. I wanted out there and then, but suddenly he threw himself on his knees in tears, begging me to stay, promising he'd never do anything like it again.

You'd think that any woman brought up in a house where there is domestic violence would never make the same mistakes her mother did. Unfortunately, that just isn't true. How many other women have made the same fatal choice I did then? I looked down at this blubbering man and, like a fool, I thought, "I can't leave this guy, he's pitiful." He was so insecure, so jealous, this Granny-reared boy who never really knew if his mother loved him or not. I felt sorry for him.

You think that if you stay, you can help someone like that, that love can conquer all. He promised me he'd never lose his temper again and I was naive enough to believe him. So I stayed. Anyway, we were under contract to Warner Brothers to make this album and I felt obliged to stay; you can't piss off people like that, there's too much money involved and it's very unprofessional.

If I'd known what was in store for me, how many times that scenario of violence followed by remorse would be played out, I'd have run screaming into the night and never looked back, but that's the wonder of hindsight. That night the weather broke and there was a massive storm. And so 'Stormbringer!' was born.

I never did get to meet Dylan again but on the Monday after the gig it was a very hot day and I had to walk down to the supermarket in the village to get supplies. As I was carrying the groceries home, a car pulled up behind me. I heard a door slam, then this man came up to me, wearing a tweed jacket with leather patches on the sleeves. He didn't tell me his name but he said he was Dylan's pianist. He told me I was a great singer and that Dylan thought I didn't like him because we hadn't turned up for tea at his house on the Sunday.

Tea at the Dylans'? This was the first I'd heard about it. John had obviously been too jealous to tell me we'd been invited there. I was raging. Then the pianist suddenly noticed the bruise under my eye. I had to explain I was married to a jealous, insecure boy and asked him to tell Dylan that was why we hadn't made it to tea. The man went on to ask me my parents' names and my birthday and he seemed very excited when I said I was Jewish. It was a strange thing to be having this conversation like this, and it ended up with my sending Dylan my good wishes and the man leaving.

When I got back to the house I asked John about the invitation and he claimed he'd forgotten to tell me. As if. It was so silly of him to miss out on an invitation like that. At the Playhouse concert John had done a wonderful version of 'Don't Think Twice' and I'm sure Dylan would have loved to use him, to play with him. When we returned to England, John would boast to journalists how we'd had tea with Bob Dylan but his insecurity couldn't let it happen for real. John was a great guitarist but Dylan would always be the number one writer and John couldn't cope with that.

We had to contact Dylan again when we had a telegram from Blackhill Enterprises, asking us to get in touch with him and invite him to play at the Isle of Wight festival that August. We found him in the Woodstock phone book under Zimmerman and he agreed to do it, but I didn't get to talk to him that time either. There wasn't another chance after that. Dylan's wife decided that the house was too dangerous for the children because it was perched on the side of a hilly mountain and they packed up and moved somewhere else, leaving Happy and Artie Traum to look after the empty house. Dylan did send us a message, however, offering us the use of his pool while he was gone, which was a thoughtful thing for him to do.

So we finally saw the house, even though the man himself wasn't there. It was beautiful, all wood, like a ski lodge, with this natural pool with lilies in it. Everyone went skinny dipping, but that wasn't my scene, so I slipped off to look inside the house and found my way down to his recording studio, where I sat alone, soaking up the atmosphere.

We never did go to the Woodstock festival, though I think John wanted to. We had my small son with us and I felt it was no place to take a baby. This was still 1969, the year that the Americans had landed on the moon and the Manson Family committed their murders. Suddenly America wasn't happy with bare-footed hippy types. Most cafes had signs saying "No bare feet" or "No hippies". We were in the countryside and everyone had a gun. I saw what it was like to live in rural middle-class America and it was totally alien to me. I'd had enough. I didn't feel safe there. I had a small child to protect and I just wanted to get back to England. I loved the forests and woodlands in the US but anything could happen there and I was ready to return to Hampstead, which seemed like Toy Town in comparison.

CHAPTER 5

London – Hastings 1969-1972

The album worked out wonderfully well, although it had gradually stopped being my album and become a John and Beverley Martyn project. That didn't worry me because we were a
couple and I thought we would promote the album as a couple.
It was a joy to work with Joe Boyd, who is a great producer,
and I was really excited by what we had created, but when we
got home and it was time for us to go on the 'Stormbringer!'
tour, things started to go bad.

Joe wanted us to tour with Fairport Convention but it
seems Sandy Denny wasn't at all happy about that. I don't like
to speak ill of the dead, but it was as if she really didn't want
me around. I was taken aback by her attitude. I think she
felt that I was a threat to her crown as THE folk singer, but
I didn't even want to be that sort of folk singer. When 'Stormbringer!' came out, she actually phoned me up and gave me a
mouthful of abuse. Incredible. The one or two times I did gig
with Fairport, she insisted on knowing in advance what I was
going to wear on stage, afraid perhaps that I would upstage
her. She was quite happy to have John there, but me she did-
n't want around. John seemed content with this arrangement,
so rather than cause any more bad feelings I stopped touring.
Perhaps I should have fought my corner more, but I have
always believed in love as the greatest power in the world and
have probably been too soft for my own good in the face of
other people's ruthlessness, so I didn't.

Then Warner Brothers wanted to put out one of my tracks from the album I had written ('Can't Get the One I Want To') as a single because they thought it would be commercially successful in the States, but John freaked out at this idea because he hadn't had a lot of input into it, so poor Joe had to go back to Warner Brothers and tell them they couldn't release it. Art Garfunkel also wanted to buy the song and do a cover version of it, but John wouldn't let that happen either. I wanted my marriage to work and so I let John dictate the terms. Looking back, it was the end of my career really, but at the time I didn't realise it.

We had started on our second album, 'Road to Ruin' as soon as we got back to England and John took control from the word go. He already wanted to be a solo artist and he kept telling Joe how to produce the album. Joe lost interest in the project because of this big man-child who kept kicking off; they were ego-battling all the time. If Joe said he wanted me to sing lead vocal, John would argue and insist he did it. Everybody gave in to John because he was big and would just kick off until he got his own way. No-one could control him. But there hadn't been any more domestic violence incidents, that is until an American couple came to stay with us in Hampstead that Christmas, and the woman dropped a remark about how you could see that Joe adored me by the way he looked at me when I was singing. John blew up and stormed off to Joe's office with a hatchet under his arm – literally. He was only stopped on the way by an old friend who managed to calm him down and take him home.

This was the sort of man I was living with. I never knew what he would do from one minute to the next. And I never realised what a drinker he was, as ridiculous as that sounds. He had been drinking since he was fourteen and I had no idea. Glasgow is a tough town to grow up in and because of that it can give you an ideal start for the music business. John became a shark among sharks. He may have looked young and pretty and soft, but inside he had to be a guy. That's what he thought being a guy was, a bit of a geezer, a hard man. He was Jekyll and Hyde, and I was only now beginning to realise it. It was alcohol that brought out his dark side.

He didn't drink in the house much in those early days, though, it was all social drinking before and after gigs or out in pubs where he'd gather an audience around him. He loved to socialise and be the centre of attention but we rarely went out together any more. Of course, I had a small child to look after, but it was as if I was banished to the house while he continued to be out living the life and going on tour.

When it came to making 'Road to Ruin', John was so controlling that Joe took to sitting in the studio reading The New York Times and The Guardian, showing no interest in what we were doing. There was no magic. It was ridiculous. Everything was moving away from me. John had come into all this as my guitarist and now he had taken over to such an extent that I felt I was being pushed out of everything.

To be fair, John had taken on another man's son and treated him like his own but he insisted on controlling everything, especially the music - and the money. It seems incredible now as I think about it, but I never had any money of my own. If I wanted anything, even food, I had to ask John and so it went on for the next ten years. If I kept my mouth shut and behaved, I might get a little reward. He kept his hands firmly on the purse strings and I didn't even begin to receive any royalties until 1975. Even then, I never got my full entitlement.

It is only recently that I have discovered that when I signed for the rights to the songs that John and I wrote together, he put himself down for 75% of the royalties and me for only 25%. He did that without telling me. I didn't actually get to read the contract at all. He thrust this piece of paper in front of me and told me where to sign. Nor did he or anyone else let me know that I should have become a member of the Performing Rights Society as he had. That would have protected my interests better and I would have benefitted from my writing more.

My trouble was that I was interested in making music, not in the contracts. And I had faith in people. It's amazing I got anything out of my songs at all, I was such easy pickings for the vultures in the music business. Over the years there were songs that John and I wrote together that I never got credited for. They would come out of our late night jamming sessions and when something began to crystallise into something I would say, "Please remember that I helped you to write this" and he'd say, "Yeah yeah. I'll do something about that" but he never did. If I pushed the issue, he'd get mad and call me a 'greedy Jewish bitch' and demand to know if I thought he didn't provide well enough for the family. They say that Marianne Faithfull wrote 'Sister Morphine' and the Rolling Stones didn't credit her for it but gave her a lump sum instead 'to save her from the tax man'.[72] It would have been nice if John had at least done something like that for me, but he didn't.

In 1971 I gave birth to my second child and John's first, his daughter. He'd been pressuring me about giving him a child and I'd been trying to put it off, but I was so worn down by the drudgery of the life I was leading that I finally gave in. I had no career to speak of. Neither did Nick Drake, who was living nearby in Belsize Park. We saw a lot of him because we lived so close and he became a good friend to us both. We let him come over to our flat whenever he wanted and I'd feed him or we'd all play cards together. Sometimes he'd use John's reel-to-reel tape recorder to put down some music while he was there.

We'd heard some of his new album when we'd come home from America and loved it but he was too lacking in confidence and too fragile to push like you have to in the music business. It was interesting to watch John and Sandy Denny, two people driven by the desire to succeed and bent on self-destruction.[73]

---

[72]**Marianne Faithfull** (b1946) A singer, actress and songwriter, she is still probably best known as Mick Jagger's girlfriend from 1966-1970.

[73]**Sandy Denny** (1947-1978) Folk rock vocalist and member of Fairport Convention.

They could both drink anyone under the table, but Nick could never be like that and he started to slip into a deep depression. He wasn't taking care of himself and he lost that beautiful glow of his and became a shabby, shuffling figure. His moods began to affect me, because we saw so much of each other and I was so dissatisfied with my life, feeling so cheated.

Of course, like so many women then, I thought it was wrong to put myself first, I should be thinking of the child or John so I just carried on. But what was it all for? I had made this wonderful album 'Stormbringer!' but I'd got nothing from it. I'd see the album in the shops with my picture on it and it was like looking at another person. What had been the point of making it if I wasn't out there gigging with John? He was becoming more and more famous while I was stuck with a small child in a tiny one bed roomed flat, seeing hardly anybody except John and Nick, the world forgetting about me.

I wasn't happy with my vocals on my two tracks of 'Road to Ruin' and I felt Joe didn't care anymore and wanted to teach me a lesson as if to say "You got into this shit because you let men walk all over you." Then, out of the blue, he announced he was going back to the States to work on the Jimi Hendrix film 'Rainbow Bridge' for Warner Brothers. The office was going to be closed; we weren't going to have a manager or a producer, although we would still be recording with Island Records. Joe asked me how I saw my career going in the future and I said I didn't know. Who could see the future? He also asked me who had written most of 'Aunty Aviator'. Well, John had given me the first line and that had given me the idea but I'd come up with the rest of it.

I think he was trying to remind me of who I was musically, but I didn't really understand what was happening. I suspected that deals were being made behind my back. I think now that everybody but me could see that John didn't want me to have a career. Why? Who knows? Jealousy? Machismo? Because I had two children by now?

Any woman with children can do at least ten quality gigs a year and still have plenty of time to spend with the kids, but I was being denied even that much. I was exhausted living in that tiny flat, stuck on my own all day with two little ones while John was out and about building his reputation; we didn't even have a garden for the children to play in. Something had to change or I would be overwhelmed. I decided it was time to get out of London.

I realised by now that John was drinking too much and dabbling with all available drugs – this was Swinging London, after all – and he was never the man to help with child-rearing. Even when he came to the hospital when I was having the baby I wanted him to leave quickly because he was so obviously uncomfortable with the situation and so unsupportive. He didn't really want to leave London – he was having a great time, but I insisted and in 1972 John found us a house in Hastings through some friends of his.

I liked being near the sea. There I could breathe fresh air and get my head together. I started practising yoga, much to John's contempt. He was always wanting to do stuff like that but never getting round to it. He was happy spending his time in London, staying with friends, but when he did come down after being on the road, he'd be like a paranoid dog, sniffing round, demanding who had been in his territory.

I was never unfaithful to John because I was terrified of him. He'd say things like, "Curse the man that takes you away." He always said he'd kill me or kill us both if I went off with anyone else – he was such a dramatic character that I believed him and didn't even want to take the chance; the risks were too great. By now things were getting so bad, that I would get myself into a state of fear and panic when he was around. I never knew what he was going to do next. I was living on my nerves. I never deliberately did anything to set him off but he would start drinking somewhere then come home and slur off into that Glaswegian accent of his, getting darker and darker. This was when the violence really began to escalate. Even now I can't think about it too much or I plunge back into depression.

There was one thing that was always good in our relationship and that was when we played music together – that was magical, mystical even.

I had never seen anyone so wrapped up in his playing, so concentrated as John. Sometimes we'd just look at each other and wonder where the music came from. It was very special and we knew it, neither of us had heard music like that before, it was almost spiritual. At those times there would be a good feeling about John and I seemed to calm him down a lot, but not when he was drinking. Sadly I couldn't always keep up with the moment. Our sessions were usually in the wee small hours of the night, and I had to get some sleep or I couldn't look after the children the next day. These sessions went on throughout our marriage; we always made great music together although gradually that really close bond we had disappeared.

I hadn't recorded anything since 'Road to Ruin' and eventually I told John I wanted to do another album. He said he'd see about it, but he came home and woke me up at 3 am in the morning to tell me that they didn't want an album from me, they only wanted one from him. It broke my heart.

He had success, but he couldn't handle it. The more he worked, the fewer were the tender moments between us. It was as if he believed he really were some Luciferian character. He changed, his outlook on life had changed. In the mid-'70s he really tried to change his image. He decided he had to move away from that hippie child look and he started getting more masculine, wearing suits like a well-dressed villain, Crombie coats and all.[74] No more cheesecloth and muslin and curly hair. That's when he grew the famous beard. It was as if he'd looked through a glass darkly. He became debauched. I didn't want to be like that. Anyway, I had the children to worry about.

---

[74]**Crombie.** Makers of classic luxury clothes since 1805.

We never were a celebrity couple in the way they exist today. John didn't use a publicity agent or employ a P.A. and he never pretended to be anyone he wasn't. His devoted fans may have believed he really was the person who came over in his songs, but they didn't know what was happening at home. Later, as he drank more and took more drugs, the chaos would spill over into his performances, which sometimes became erratic and shambolic, and he developed a reputation as a hell-raiser.

John even got into trouble with the law again. He'd been violent towards a sailor on a train and received a suspended sentence for GBH. But I knew nothing about this. He was a rising star on Island Records, the label that would later bring Bob Marley to the world's notice, and I believe people there decided not to tell me to protect their interests. I'm not talking about the head of Island, Chris Blackwell. I always found him a good man, but others who must have had some idea of what was happening to me preferred to keep quiet. I might have been able to escape if people who should have known better hadn't kept secrets from me.

If I'd known about the suspended sentence, I might have had some defence against John. I could've called the police when he attacked me and he would probably have been banged up. I don't know if I ever would have done that, but I would have had a choice. Like most battered wives, I was too ashamed to tell anybody what was happening. Only the doctor in Hastings knew the full extent of my injuries and he was silenced by the Hippocratic Oath; at times I thought I was going to die.

Fortunately, John wasn't actually at home a lot of the time we were married. He was out playing and being the star while I was left with the babies. The beach was only minutes from our front door and the children and I spent some golden days down there. I would make a picnic and we'd spend all day outside. The children would be splashing about in the water and I would just lie there, soaking up the sun. When John was there, it was like you were on an adrenalin rush all the time. You knew that you had to fit into his lifestyle. What he wanted to eat had to be got in and it had to be cooked just as he wanted and it had to be just right. If he had to go off again it was my job to get his clothes ready.

For John, a woman's place was tending her man, who was the most important person in the family. It was if I existed merely to serve him and to bring up our children. I do believe he loved me, but in the only way he knew how to, which was always putting himself first, probably because he'd already been broken-hearted by his mother. I knew from early on that he wasn't faithful to me. There'd be women with names like Morning Star ringing from LA asking 'if John Martyn were there'. I felt like Joan Baez after Dylan dumped her, his having done very well out of the association, thank you very much.[75]

The first time I had seen John's madness was that night in Woodstock, but it began to appear more and more frequently. There would be gaps and then something would trigger him off again and there'd be another episode of violence followed by remorse. Each time he would say that wasn't really him and he would never do it again and by now I was too shell-shocked and isolated to do anything but accept his apologies. The gaps between the episodes got to be less and less as he started to hang out with more and more villains. I'm not mentioning any names, but these were people who could get you a gun if you wanted one or a bag of coke. They weren't musicians but they loved John's music. I think he enjoyed hanging out with gangster types. He loved the romance of it all and saw himself as a sort of Jesse James figure, fighting against the establishment and all that.

There were a lot of times when he wasn't there and I could actually calm down and be myself and live a normal sort of life but when he was home I had to watch everything I said and did around him. Living like that, you gradually get used to being treated like a beaten dog. You cower as if you expect bad

---

[75]**Joan Baez** (b1941) Folk singer and activist, she helped bring Bob Dylan's songs to public notice.

things. I remember many times hearing him come into the kitchen and never knowing if there was going to be a knife against my throat because the children were making too much noise and he wanted to sleep. You had to think about all those things all the time. It gradually began to take a toll on my health, both mental and physical.

It was in Hastings that I realised that John had been dabbling in the occult since he was a kid. When I met him, he had a collection of books by Aleister Crowley.[76] I'd never heard of the man and was curious so I asked John about him, but he just brushed me off with, "Oh, it's not for women." Then one day in Hastings, I overheard a tour guide say: "And here we have the house of the famous wizard, Aleister Crowley", pointing at the house two doors down from ours, "He was reputed to be the most wicked man in Europe." Apparently, there were caves beneath these houses that had devils painted on the walls. I was stunned. I knew nothing about the Black Arts and suchlike, and here I was, married to an acolyte of Crowley's, the man who misused the Wiccan Law of "Do what thou wilt, so long as ye harm none", changing it to "Do what thou wilt shall be the whole of the law." Years later I discovered that Crowley's teachings were very popular with a lot of ambitious young men in the music business, Led Zeppelin among them. I never saw John running around in long black robes or biting the heads off chickens, but he certainly didn't mind who he trampled on in his rise to fame. I don't know whether the move to Hastings was a coincidence or a result of the Crowley connection, but his career definitely developed while we lived there.

John loved being noticed and would spend hours in the Hastings pubs, telling stories to a bunch of piss artists then bringing them all back home to party on in our house; uncouth people, who'd pull down their trousers and show you the

---

[76]**Aleister Crowley** (1875-1947) Black Magician and Satanist who identified himself with the notorious 666, the number of the Antichrist.

tattoos on their arses, town slappers who'd had a kiss and a cuddle with him when he was drunk. It was horrible. It was as if he didn't see me as a person. I grew terrified of him.

No matter how I tried to please him or placate him, this nasty, vicious side would eventually come out. I truly believe he was taking out his anger with his mother on me. I couldn't leave. I had nowhere to go and no money to go with. Anyway, marriage was for life. That's what I believed. And I was in denial about the violence. I can only say that as a battered wife I felt disgusted with myself that I let it happen, or that I tolerated this behaviour for so long. I thought this was normal, this was how marriage was. It had been like this for my mother and now it was the same for me. Domestic violence wasn't as recognised then as it is now. And like any abused woman, I thought it must somehow have been my fault. That's how crazy wife-beating can turn you.

John was an angry man. The only time I ever saw him peaceful was when he was playing music or sitting on a riverbank, fishing. I think some of his anger was guilt at his treatment of me. He'd killed my career, he'd killed me, really and then he had to come home and see what he'd done to me. It seemed so unfair. He was gathering praise and adulation while I was disappearing into nothingness.

For John the adoration of strangers was an addiction. People who wouldn't have given him the time of day if they'd known what he was really like were the stuff of life to him. In truth he was a bully. He bullied women half his size who couldn't defend themselves. If I complained about his hitting me he'd growl, "Do you want another one?" And he would tell me to do things that weren't right, business things. He promised me a recording deal, but nothing came of it.

John was too clever to sign any of his rights away, but I never developed a head for business; I never got a handle on my dyscalculia and numbers stayed a mystery to me. At one time there was a bit of money put up for me to make an album, but I never saw any of it. I recorded the songs, good songs using samba and reggae, songs before their time, but to this day I've never even seen the masters and the album was never released. It was as if no-one was taking me seriously. I was just this woman having babies. When 'I don't wanna know about evil' came out of a jamming session between me and John he refused to put my name on it. He had started playing a rhythm, and I came out with the first two lines: "I don't wanna know about evil, I just wanna know about love." That's what it was like all the time. He was always promising me that I'd do something one day, but it never happened.

You never imagine that the person you are married to could behave like that. He did whatever it took to take his career a massive leap forward; I am not the only person to have been crushed down on their partner's way to the top. Why did I tolerate the abuse for so long? I loved him and I realised he wasn't well, that he had a problem. I wanted to make things better for him but what he needed was professional help. All I could do was be there and become a whipping boy for him. No-one in their right mind wants to get whipped but when you let yourself get dragged into that sort of relationship you can end up losing your own life force, your belief in yourself.

CHAPTER 6

Hastings – Jamaica – Heathfield 1972-1979

Over the years John put me down so often that I felt like nothing. He'd tell me I couldn't play, that I didn't even know how to tune a guitar properly and yet he still wanted to make music with me and share my bed. It was a strange existence and I felt quite punch drunk at times and unable to hold things together. I was getting more and more abuse and becoming more and more like a dog, cowering in the corner.

It was in the early '70s that our marriage really began to crumble when Island Records decided it would be a good idea to get John working with Claire Hamill.[77] She was a young folk singer, their new signing, and he played on her first two albums. She then went on tour with him as his supporting artist. I was gutted by all this. John and I had made these two marvellous albums together yet he didn't want to play with me professionally anymore; he was supposed to be going solo and here he was linking up with some other woman. I suppose I was jealous because I was sure there was something going on between them besides music, although John kept denying it, even swearing on his children's lives that nothing was happening. The funny thing was that at the same time as he was insisting there was nothing between him and Claire, he couldn't come near me

---

[77]**Claire Hamill** (b1954) Writer of the song 'You Take My breath Away'.

sexually because he'd caught something really nasty. In spite of this, I was still supposed to believe his protestations. It tore our marriage apart because he was so unsettled.

Sometime in the late '90s, I did a gig on the same bill as Claire Hamill at The Mean Fiddler in Oxford St. London. I said to a friend of mine who had come to watch the show: "I'm certain this woman had something sexual going on with John in the '70s." When Claire came into my dressing room after the show, all hugs and kisses, she said how she'd always wanted to meet me. I didn't say anything, but my pal, who by now had had a drink or three, immediately blurted out: "Did you have a scene with John Martyn?" Claire denied anything had happened and quickly left the room, whereupon my pal muttered "Guilty", with a knowing wink in her eye. I finally found out the apparent truth when I read John Munroe's biography of John in 2007. In that, Claire admitted to having an affair with John. I knew my intuition had been right all along!

But back in the '70s, the party that was our life when John was home was getting crazier and crazier and the only time I had anything remotely like a normal life was when he was away for weeks on tour, and even then I was too afraid to make many new friends. Nick Drake was one of the few people allowed to visit me. He would turn up all the time. If he came down when John wasn't there I would feed him up and he would sit, drinking tea and looking out at the sea for hours. We had a young girl staying with us at that time named Teresa May. She was the daughter of some people we knew and she was living with us because she didn't want to board at her convent school. Who can blame her? She was happy to babysit for me, so sometimes in the evening, when the children were asleep, Nick and I we would go for a drink or take my dog Albert for a walk.

Albert was this lovely cross breed Scots Collie and Labrador, all black and shaggy. I had him for about three years but then we had to let him go to a farm because the neighbours complained so much about his barking every time someone walked past our door.

On other evenings Nick and I would sit and play music together. We started writing a song together called 'Reckless Jane', which I finished writing only about two years ago. Sometimes when I went to visit my sister in Coventry, Nick would be staying with his family in the nearby village of Tanworth-in-Arden and we would meet up somewhere for a coffee. He once asked me to go and meet his mother and father, but I talked it over with my sister and we decided it wouldn't really be the right thing to do, seeing as I was married to John, although my friendship with Nick was never anything but a friendship.

The last time I saw Nick, I was pregnant again. He and John had been out together and when they came back, Nick seemed to be in a bad mood. John went into the kitchen and started cooking, and I heard Nick say: "I always trusted you, John, but now I see you're really devious." Then he asked me if I thought John was devious. I couldn't answer his question, and certainly not in front of John. I'd never seen Nick like this before. He was always such a romantic, gentle man, and here he was being angry and confrontational with me, as if he'd seen something in John he hadn't known was there and was now challenging me to look closely at the man I'd married.

He'd seen John doing things such as flicking me with tea towels in the past and he always left the house when anything like that happened but now it was as if John had said or done something that night that really upset him. Then Nick asked me: "What do you think of me?" Before I had time to answer him, John shouted from the kitchen: "She fucking loves you, man. She's always worried about you." By now I'd had enough. The pregnancy was making me feel sick to my stomach and I couldn't handle whatever was going on, so I made my excuses and went to bed.

It didn't worry me to leave John and Nick together. I knew John would never hurt Nick, he loved him and treated him like a younger brother. John would have killed anyone else who'd dared to call him devious, but with Nick he was always gentle.

The next morning I made Nick marmalade on toast and a cup of tea. He was very sullen and didn't want to speak. When he got up to go, I went to hug him but he pushed me away. That was the last time I saw him. He was dead eight weeks later. Shortly before he died, I received a phone call from his mother, Molly, telling me that Nick wanted to see me. She asked me if I could go up to Tanworth-in-Arden but I explained about my pregnancy and said I didn't think I could handle the journey. In my heart, I didn't think I could handle the emotion either, the way I was feeling. She then asked if John could go instead. He was happy to do that and immediately headed up to the Midlands for a few days.

When he came back, he told me that Nick was in a bad way, that there was nothing anyone could do to help him. Nick was very, very low. He had wanted to make up his friendship with us and apologised for that last evening. With hindsight, it was as if he was tying up the loose ends in his life. I was glad we were all friends again but I felt that he was going to do something bad. I told John I thought we were going to lose him but it still came as a shock when the phone rang and I watched John's stricken face as the news was broken to him. When he put the phone down he said: "He did it" and walked out of the house. I didn't see him for the next two days. He was off dealing with his grief in his way, leaving me alone to deal with mine.

I never really knew what Nick had meant by his question to me that evening: "What do you think of me?" but he had done a great thing for me. He had shown himself to be a true friend by confronting John and that had somehow given me hope that I wasn't so alone. Now he was gone.

Whether Nick overdosed deliberately or accidentally we'll never know. He was a public schoolboy and a university graduate who had been born with a silver spoon in his mouth. He'd never been comfortable out in the real world where Glaswegian bruisers like John ruled the roost. I was grief-stricken by his death. I'd had the feeling something bad was going to happen, but nobody was helping him, he was too sick to reach, and in those days, there was an even greater stigma attached to mental illness than there is today; there just weren't enough professionals around to help.

I think his family needed to think it was an accident. I thought he'd had enough and the pain, whatever it was, was too much. But it all adds to the value of the myth. It's a cruel thing to say, but I think there were people who exploited his death. There weren't that many around when he was alive, just a couple of good friends. That beautiful young man on the album sleeve didn't last for long. He became all wrapped up inside and we lost him in late 1974, six months before our youngest son was born.

It was perhaps partly in response to that loss that another doomed young man came into our lives around this time. John had worked with Paul Kossoff on his solo album 'Back Street Crawler' back in 1973 and held him in great respect as an artist.[78] But Paul was a sensitive Jewish boy masquerading as the wild man of rock and by 1975 he was in drug rehab for his addictions. I believe he was also hurt by his father's disapproval of his rock and roll lifestyle. It's hard when your father is a very well-respected, respectable actor and you have re-invented yourself as a drug-addicted rocker. I remember Paul would sit in the kitchen, clutching a glass of *crème de menthe frappe* in his hand, that green liqueur with ice and soda he was so fond of, telling tales of his old Jewish grandmother 'with her gnarled hands'. I was very fond of him, but I sensed that we were in danger of losing him too. He had actually died for several minutes when his heart stopped beating while he was in rehab. They brought him back, but only four weeks later he was out on tour with John, drinking and taking drugs again. Much too soon. The tour reinvigorated Paul, at least temporarily, but sadly, his playing was too

---

[78]**Paul Kossoff** (1950 - 1976). Lead guitarist of the band Free and guitarist on their classic 'All Right Now'. Son of well-known British actor David Kossoff.

erratic for John to include his tracks on the album he put out after the tour.

This was the 'white' album, 'Live at Leeds', that had been the last but one gig of the tour.[79] It was a period of total madness for me because John decided to put the album out himself. Somehow, a coupon got printed with our home address on it and a lot of people started sending postal orders for £3 to get a copy signed by John. I would have to sort out the post as it came in and write down the orders in a book and do all the practical business of mailing out the records because John had promptly gone off on another tour! He was away most of the time, as usual, and I was having to handle all this by myself as well as look after two small children and a new baby.

All sorts of weird individuals began turning up at the house because John had put the address out on the advert for the album, adding to the strain. By time all the albums had been sold and posted, I was totally worn out. John also wanted to get away for a time, so he decided we'd all go to Jamaica for a couple of months. He'd arranged it with Chris Blackwell of Island records and we were going to stay in his house, Strawberry Hill, the idea being that it would be a good rest for us all. So off we went to Jamaica *en famille*.

Jamaica is a stunning island, so rich and fertile, and Blackwell's house was also amazing. It lay about 15 miles from Kingston, up this dirt track of a mountain road. It was an original plantation house with lots of land and outbuildings where the staff lived. There was Agnes who cooked for us and her son who looked after the grounds. I believe the house had to be rebuilt after Hurricane Gilbert in 1988 so perhaps it isn't as beautiful now as it once was, but then it was old Colonial style with wooden shutters. The air up the mountain was clean and beautiful, so you really felt like the gods looking down on the city of Babylon, or Kingston to the locals.

---

[79]'Live at Leeds' was released in 1976.

It was a wonderful place for children. The kids loved it there. They would hunt for these big red and yellow caterpillars in the lush garden or go looking for humming birds. My youngest was extremely underweight when we arrived and Agnes taught me how to make cornmeal porridge to build him up. It worked. We didn't want her to go to any trouble on our behalf and told her we were happy to eat whatever everyone else ate. This turned out to be chicken and rice, which seemed to be the staple diet wherever you went.

You couldn't help but feel better in such a glorious place but I was very quiet there – feeling abused, being withdrawn, not having a character anymore, as if I didn't even know what my own identity was. Looking back, I suppose it was the beginning of my break-down. I seemed to be living through John, it was his trip and he was the star. Unfortunately, even in Jamaica John would have his usual episodes and again everyone around was careful not to mention my tell-tale bruises. But it was a holiday. And the sunshine was incredible.

John loved it. He would terrorise the local population by going into town and drinking white rum then sounding off in his broad accent, reminding the islanders of a Scottish dragoon who took Kingston apart the day the British left the island.

At one point we went down to Nassau in the Bahamas where Chris had a guest house and his wife took us out in a speed boat to Compass Point. Back on Jamaica we went to meet Lee 'Scratch' Perry, the dub king, at the recording studio he had in his back garden, known as the Black Ark. There he created so many innovative sounds and recording techniques for artists such as his own band The Upsetters and later, Bob Marley; he was at the heart of the new *ska, reggae* and later, *dancehall* recordings.

Both Scratch and John loved the echoplex, a machine designed to achieve delay effects in music. John had taken his to Jamaica with him so he and Scratch sat and played together happily; I have an idea some of their music may have gone out locally at that time, but I'm not 100% sure about that.

Scratch was an amazing man but somewhat strange. He was a genius in the studio but he'd also smoked a lot of *ganja* in his time. Whatever the reason, he was given to making bizarre pronouncements when you least expected them. He once called Chris Blackwell a vampire and said he'd seen him drink the blood of chickens, but I don't think there was any evidence. Legend has it that he burnt his own studio down in 1979 to get rid of the 'unclean spirits' there, although some of his family insist the fire was caused by an electrical fault during renovations in 1983.

Scratch and his wife came to stay with us in England a couple of years later when we were living in the country. He regularly went running round the block and wore blue silk running shorts and a vest the entire time he was with us. He ate nothing but ice-cream, although he enjoyed helping to prepare food for the rest of us. He and John wrote a song together then called Big Muff, about a particular sort of fuzz box; the name made Scratch laugh because of its sexual connotations. He was a very well-behaved house guest and he loved watching the wrestling on the TV – in particular, Haystack and Big Daddy - exclaiming "Al-migh-ty" at the television screen repeatedly in that Jamaican drawl of his.

One afternoon in Jamaica John and I met up with Chris Blackwell in Kingston and he asked John if he could take me shopping. As we went off, he handed me a big brown bag. I had a peek inside and it was full of American dollars. With me clutching the bag, we took off to the roughest parts of Kingston where he'd buy up any ancient hand-painted postcards of old Jamaica he could find. He'd make the deal in the local patois and then I'd hand over the money. We never had any trouble with the locals, maybe because neither of us was particularly dressed up that day and when we'd finished he gave me a handful of the postcards to take home with me, which I later enjoyed sending off to various people.

Another time he and John were playing poker together in some hotel or other in Kingston and I was just sitting around watching the game. Blackwell ordered tea and toast for me, which was a thoughtful thing to do. He seemed a very gentle guy. He asked me if I were comfortable up at Strawberry Hill and I assured him I was. It would have been hard not to be comfortable there; it was where Bob Marley went to recuperate when he got shot in 1976.

At that time Chris was planning to make *reggae* known to the world so there was this sort of reggae convention going on in various venues around Jamaica. Every musician on the island came out of the woodwork. When we went to the Black Ark, there were hundreds of them sitting on the walls outside, some with goats tethered by them, some conducting *ganja* deals while they waited, as women walked along with bales of bananas on their heads. It was crazy and fascinating. We'd be booked into these fancy hotels in different seaside resorts and we'd get to hear all the reggae bands from that part of the island, which was a marvellous experience. Chris knew this music was going to go out into the world, even back to Africa where it had originally come from and the atmosphere was incredible. We were so lucky to be witnesses to this moment of musical history.

Of course a holiday wouldn't be a holiday without a crisis. Ours occurred when our youngest son developed a stomach infection, perhaps from bad water from the water tank that served Strawberry Hill, and he was really poorly. We decided the best thing would be to take him down to the hospital in Kingston but John wouldn't go with me. I had to get a taxi by myself down into the city, which was really quite scary; Kingston was the only truly crazy place I saw in Jamaica. Fortunately, my son didn't have to be admitted so after they treated him I could take him back up the mountain the same day, medicine in my purse.

It was the news of Paul Kossoff's death that brought us back to England in March 1976. He'd had a drug-induced heart attack on a plane going to Los Angeles. He was only 25.

Coming back to an English winter was awful. I couldn't understand why we were living in a place where there were only a few days of sunshine a year. We started dreaming about retiring to Jamaica one day. I got quite down about it, especially as Hastings had become a non-stop party, with hangers-on banging on our door day and night. There was no privacy. John was drinking and partying all the time. He was a celebrity in Hastings, but my life was very lonely.

And so, in 1976, we moved to Heathfield, a quiet country town in Sussex, where we first rented, then bought a big beautiful detached house called Kenana. It had the county's only Douglas fir tree in the front garden and I loved living there. There was a large garden for the children and it should have been idyllic. But for me it became hell.

With more and more booze and drugs came more and more violence. Over the years I received a broken nose, a fractured inner ear and hairline fractures of the skull. One night he smashed a chair over me and my arm was damaged when I put it up to protect my head from the force of the blow. John wouldn't even let me call a doctor, let alone go to the hospital. A woman friend came round and was horrified to see the state of me. She helped me wrap my arm up as best we could and it eventually mended on its own, but there are still several scars and a crater near my elbow where it was hit and it always gives me gyp to this day. "Get back into bed", he'd snarled, "or I'll throw the baby out of the window". That was the sort of stupid thing John would do and say.

The two youngest children were still not old enough at this point to really understand what was happening, but my eldest son was beginning to be aware of things. Although he didn't have a clear memory of that night, years later he told me how he was reminded of it when he saw a film in which a man threatened to throw a baby out of a window. It brought the whole sorry incident back to him in a flash and he had to leave the cinema.

Another time John came back with a gun in a holster and I freaked because I thought it was a real gun. He claimed it was a starter pistol but I couldn't trust him and I couldn't get near enough to see for myself. It was all mind games like that, playing on my vulnerability. I didn't know how I'd ever get away from him safely. I was so afraid he would hurt anyone I turned to for help.

I could have gone to a battered wives' home, but I'd heard stories about places like that and could just imagine John arriving at the door of one and trying to break in, creating hell for all the other women there. He didn't know his own strength. I'd have bruises on the tops of my arms, my chin – he was constantly smacking me under the mouth so that I would bite my tongue. It was always, "Sit down. Shut up". And he was such a jealous man. There were arguments about what I was wearing. He'd accuse me of trying to attract other men. Too much eye makeup or not enough. Wear this kohl, put this henna on your hair, don't wear this, do wear that. He would choose what clothes I went out in. I had to be covered, nothing sexy. I wasn't even allowed to wear trousers, I must've looked too good in them. He had me in great long Bedouin dresses with clogs on my feet – not great for going up and down stairs with children in my arms. He'd come back from tour and inspect the house, saying things like, "Who moved that?" "Who put that blind up?" as if I had this secret handyman stashed away, some guy who would slip in when he wasn't there.

Even when he wasn't hitting me, his voice and manner would be very threatening; even when he was pretending it frightened me. I would get palpitations from fear. I eventually got used to the physical pain but it was the mental pain that was worse, the constant putting down. Words can be a weapon of abuse, whatever the old adage about 'sticks and stones...' might say. He'd even make anti-Semitic remarks to me. "Take your fat Jewish arms off me" was one of them. I was pregnant with his second child that time. Nobody needs to hear stuff like that when they're pregnant.

He wanted it so that no-one else would fancy me. He had to be in control. He intimidated me about everything. I see now what an insecure bully he was, what a classic wife-beater, but in the middle of it all I was so squashed as a human being, I thought it must have been my fault. I was so frightened all the time; I didn't even dare to make any friends.

I'm sure his pain was there long before I met him. He knew for a long time there was something not right with him. He would sing about it – "I'll take your sadness and make it mine and leave my madness in your mind" – but the only time he ever went to a therapist for help, the man stupidly told him he might not play so well if he were cured so that was the end of that. He got away with it for so long because of who he was.

People labelled him 'eccentric' and he did do eccentric things. He had a whole Parma ham hanging behind a door for two years because he liked the stuff, but didn't eat any of it. He was a collector who had to surround himself with stuff and more stuff. People fill up on stuff like that because they're insecure, they feel unloved. And he did have issues with his mother that were never resolved. The only successful relationships he ever had with women were with his grandmother and our daughter, who managed to find a piece of him that she could love, in spite of everything she'd seen as a child; he was very lucky to have that, and so was she.

I think it was also because of his mother that he was so driven to be noticed. That lovely old jazz musician Chet Baker once advised, "You find something you're good at doing and then do it better than anyone else." That's what John did, but he also wanted to rub his success in his mother's face. As for Chet Baker, he developed an addiction to speed balls – heroin and cocaine mixed – and died falling out of a hotel window in Amsterdam in 1988, yet another beautiful man who'd been on a path to destruction.

The sad thing was that John had a really sweet side to him when he was sober. He once brought a tramp home and fed him up, then gave him a bath and some money to help him on his way. I think he recognised how easy it would be for him to end up like that, if he hadn't had his talent. He also had such great taste in things; he would often bring me back an item or some clothing or an ornament that was really beautiful. And he knew about food and cooking. When he'd first come to visit me in the home for unmarried mothers, he'd brought muesli, cheese and honey, delicacies to me on my limited income. He taught me how to cook curries and stews, though he'd stand there giving orders such as "Don't leave stuff on the stove! Don't let things burn! Always keep an eye on things!" As a result I spent half our marriage in the kitchen, or out shopping for the finest ingredients and the other half looking after small children.

Although we rarely had what you'd call a normal married life because John was away so much, he always used to make sure he had the whole of September off and we would all go up to Scotland for the month. He had an uncle who worked in the Forestry Department and he would find us a lovely cottage near some woods. We'd try and live very simply. John would go fishing for salmon and I'd cook it on an open fire. He used to take the kids fishing while I sat and painted with some beautiful water colours he bought me. We'd go looking for golden eagles and walking in the woods. He got things right occasionally, and although he was never a hands-on father he was a very affectionate man, very tactile and he would always try to make sure we all went on outings together. Those were good days. But there were too few of them.

What made it worse for me in Heathfield was that the violence was starting to affect the children. I had grown up in an atmosphere like this and now it was happening to my babies. They were old enough now to be aware of what was going on. They would be disturbed by the noises in the night and come downstairs shouting, "Daddy, Daddy, stop hurting Mummy!" just as my siblings and I had done back there in Coventry so many years before.

Why do we always repeat the abuses of our lives? I thought I'd married a man who was different from my father but he wasn't really. I of all people should have known how children can be damaged by what they see in the home and I deeply regret that some of my children's problems in adulthood are my fault, because I just couldn't get myself out of there. I was frozen with fear of how he would hurt me if I told anybody about it. It sounds unbelievable and when I look back I can hardly recognise myself as that demoralised creature. But you can be the strongest, most intelligent, most talented person in the world and still fall prey to domestic violence, perhaps because there is no logic to it, no cause and effect. It is rooted in one person's madness.

People definitely knew something of what was going on, there were tell-tale marks visible often enough, but they couldn't or they wouldn't interfere. It was 'domestic'. And John could be a scary man. No man can put himself in the role of a battered wife, although we now know that domestic violence transcends gender. But then it still happened behind closed doors and women carried the brunt of it. I had put this man up on this pedestal and eventually I had to pull him down myself and rebuild the broken pieces.

It's not that I didn't want to help him anymore, but sometimes you get so intimate with someone you almost become one with them and you lose yourself, then you're no help to anyone. And you see so much of their weakness that they keep hidden from everyone else. Whatever he saw in the world destroyed him. I've learned that if you are around people like that you get damaged yourself and to an extent the children got damaged because of what they saw. Our daughter managed to turn it into something positive but it takes a very special person to do that. I protected the children to the best of my ability from what was happening between me and their father and when I could no longer recognise any of the good things I'd seen in him, I got them away in 1979.

CHAPTER 7

Heathfield 1979-1985

I certainly didn't wake up on that last day thinking it would be the last. I remember it started quite normally, with my getting the children organised and then posting a birthday card to one of my sisters. Hamish was a very pleasant house guest. He was a warm man with a bawdy sense of humour and was staying with us because he was doing a gig nearby. I was used to cooking and having the evening meal all ready for them, but they came back from the pub so very, very late. I was just too tired to stay up any longer; I needed to sleep. Anyway, it was never comfortable being around when there was another man in the room. Other times it had happened John would suddenly accuse me or the guy of flirting and things would get ugly. So I brought the dishes in and turned to go, and that's when John laid his hands on me for the last time.

I wish I could say that life became a bed of roses from that day on. But I can't. A battered woman has to overcome her shame at being the victim before she can do anything about it and that takes time. And it can take a lot of effort to make sure you never let this person hurt you again. Just hearing John's voice on the telephone or seeing him in court would make me start shaking and my legs would turn to jelly. My blood pressure would rise, I was that terrified of him. I'm sure all this stress was at the root of my later health problems. I know I made the only sane choice by reclaiming my freedom as a human being.

I could begin to make my own choices again after I left him and I gradually started to get my inner strength back.

I believe it's only your own belief system that keeps you alive. Damaged people can be very spiteful but nobody can be that cruel to you that you don't have something of your own soul left; you don't have to turn into a monster yourself. People have gone through worse than me and survived. If they could do it, so could I.

The first thing that happened was that John had to sign an undertaking not to come back to the house, but that very night he broke in and I had to escape down the street again. This time I went to a hotel and appealed to John's manager to get me some money so I could at least look after the children. Money was always a problem. John's idea of child support was to just pay the mortgage every month, nothing more. I think it was about £150 a month. I owned half the house only because his manager at the time we were buying it had realised that I didn't have a penny to my name, and he had made sure my name was on the deeds too. But two years before the divorce went through, John stopped paying even that. I had to start claiming Social Security.

It seems that someone had advised John to move to Scotland, and for some legal reason this protected his assets all through the divorce proceedings. To this day I have never understood the ins and outs of it. I only know he fought me all the way to the divorce and I never received a penny from him. I would occasionally see figures from his accountant demonstrating how something like £100,000 a year shrank to nothing after expenses and taxes etc. My solicitor must have written him at least 150 letters over the years, all of which I had to eventually pay for. John ignored every one of them. He was a law unto himself.

Even after the separation I kept getting nasty drunken phone calls from him, usually in the middle of the night, saying things like: "Who did you leave me for?" "I left you for myself", was my reply to that. Then he'd go on and on about all the things

I'd never get from him and I would ask him why he wanted to make things so difficult for the children but he would just start rambling tearfully about 'his babies, his babies' and so it went on until I just had to leave the phone off the hook. I know the breakup was very painful for him but the marriage had become more than I could endure. I would suffer fear and panic attacks and I knew things weren't right with me, because I could feel my heart beating like it was coming out of my chest.

John actually came back to the house one afternoon in 1981. I had recently met Wilko Johnson.[80] He and I got on really well and we started playing music together. He was a happily married man with a lovely wife and he would come down to Kenana purely to make music. I always remember his story about how when he was playing with The Blockheads, they appeared on Top of the Pops, singing 'I Wanna be Straight', dressed as policemen. After the gig they all stayed in their uniforms and went to the studio where The Clash were recording and knocked on the window.[81] When the band looked up and saw all these bobby helmets lined up outside, they panicked and flushed all their drugs down the loo.

Sometimes Wilko brought other musicians with him. There was one weekend when he brought Johnny Rotten, accompanied by various members of his band and a couple of punkettes.[82] This was when Johnny had joined Public Image and had reverted to his real name, John Lydon. As they were waiting for a taxi at Etchingham station, my car having broken down again, they were approached by a policeman who asked, "Aren't you that Johnny Nasty?" "No", replied Johnny with his crate of Pils lager at his feet. "Yes, you are, you're Johnny Nasty from that punk band." "No, I'm not", insisted Johnny,

---

[80]**Wilko Johnson** (b1947) Guitarist and songwriter, played first with Dr. Feelgood (1970s) and later with Ian Dury's Blockheads.

[81]**The Clash.** English punk rock band formed in 1976.

[82]**Johnny Rotten** (b1956). British rock musician and lyricist. Lead singer of the punk band The Sex Pistols.

who was determined to be addressed only by his new name. Wilko had to stand there trying to look cool, clutching a briefcase which contained goodness knows what illegal substances until the policeman finally gave up and wandered off.

The afternoon John Martyn turned up Wilko was there with some other musicians. I think John got the wrong impression as to what was happening because he started to sound off. I suddenly remembered he still had two guns stashed away in the bedroom closet – two 12-gauge shotguns - and decided I had to get them out of the house before anything dreadful could happen. Perhaps I was being paranoid, but I think I was thinking rationally and trying to work out the best scenario for all the people around us. I managed to slip upstairs as Wilko tried to calm him down. "I know you love her, man," I heard Wilko saying, "But this isn't the way. You're doing everything wrong."

I retrieved the guns and wrapped them in a coat, then managed to slip outside and hide them in the boot of my car. As I came back into the house, I heard John slurring to the children: "Who do you want to go with, me or Mummy?" He was terrifying them, and they ran to me. I bustled them out of the house and into the car and drove off to a friend's house, where we stayed the night. I gave the guns to a farmer I knew who had his own collection safely under lock and key – he also had a licence for them, which was more than John had.

The next day the children were starting school, so I drove back to the house early. John had left the night before, but his parting present was to smear jam on every door knob in the house. And in my bed. And on my clothes. The kids were absolutely freaked out by this. It was such a childish thing to have done. What was wrong with the man? He really needed help; I don't think he always realised what he was doing. He certainly had a spiteful streak that would come out when he was drinking.

I remember once his mother had come to see him performing in a prestigious gig and he refused to meet up with her afterwards. "What do you think she wants?" he asked me. "Just to say goodbye, I would think. She's an old lady, John, what are you doing?" I couldn't understand how he wouldn't see her, but he refused and he never saw her again. He would do ridiculously stupid things like that, without thinking, and then regret them afterwards. He had a brilliant mind, but it was clouded by booze.

After we split, life was really hard. I had to survive on state benefits and the strain was enormous. I managed to get a little work – I went on a short UK tour with Loudon Wainwright III and played the main stage at Glastonbury in 1981.[83] Nick McGerr, later the manager of Brighton band Peter and the Test Tube Babies, had got me the Loudon gig and I remember we would arrive at each venue in his big old black Citroen car, which was a fun thing to do.[84]

It was an enjoyable experience working with Loudon. He was a very professional man, good humoured and very kind. If a string on my guitar broke while I was on-stage, he would be standing in the wings with his own guitar ready to pass over to me so I could carry on playing. I learnt a lot about how to present a tighter set on that tour and I was performing better and better as the tour went on. We did a week's stint at The Venue in London and for that Wilko Johnson lent me his sidemen, including Simon Climie, a multi-talented young man.[85]

Glastonbury didn't start off well. I couldn't get through all the traffic jammed around the site and I arrived late for my spot. The Thompson Twins had had to go on before me and Michael Eavis was quite angry at first but he quickly forgave me and ushered me up to the farmhouse where his wife was

---

[83]**Loudon Wainwright III** (b1946) American folk singer, songwriter, humourist and actor.

[84]**Peter and the Test Tube Babies.** Punk rock band formed in 1978.

[85]**Simon Climie** (b1957) Singer and prolific songwriter. He co-wrote 'I knew you were waiting (for me)', the duet sung by Aretha Franklin and George Michael.

cooking up a meal.[86] I saw my old friend Roy Harper there, waiting to go on for his set later that evening and it was good to see him again. I finally went on to perform at about 5pm.

The stage was still under construction when I started and the audience were still drifting in, although there were about 20 – 30,000 people there already. I opened my set with a song called 'The Ancient Wisdom'. It begins 'I was born on the banks of the river Nile' and I thought it was a suitable opening number for that pyramid stage. The audience responded well and I went on to do an hour of my own songs. I played acoustic guitar and was joined for some of the set by Mick Harradine, a young musician from Sussex, playing electric guitar. I really enjoyed doing the gig, and it was good to feel that the audience enjoyed it too.

But these were just little islands in a sea of no work. I had been out of the business for too long, and I had the day-to-day worry of supporting the children. They had to go to school in second-hand clothes and get free school dinners in this rather middle-class country area we were living in. I worried all the time about how all this was affecting them. The children never received anything from John all those years, not a present nor a card even. It wasn't that he didn't love them, I think the break-up was just too painful for him.

It wasn't until 1984, when she was thirteen that our daughter decided to go and see her father, who was playing a gig at The Dome in Brighton. John got all emotional at the sight of her and told everyone in the band that I had stopped him from seeing the children. Simply not true. The meeting went well and he sent her home with some money and a big sweater because she didn't have a proper coat; he also asked if he could see his son. My youngest son really wanted to see his father, but wasn't old enough until 1986 or 1987 when he was eleven or twelve

---

[86]**Thompson Twins.** British pop group who performed from 1977 - 1993, achieving worldwide popularity in the '80s. **Michael Eavis** (b1935) Organises and hosts Glastonbury Festival on his farm in Somerset.

and we all went to another gig of John's, also in The Dome. After that, he sent for the two children to fly up to Scotland to stay with him for a holiday. My eldest son was happily developing a life for himself and had no interest in rekindling his relationship with his step-father, but the two youngest had always longed to see their dad again.

I was glad that the children were seeing their father but it made no difference to my dire financial needs. As the weeks turned into months and then years and the situation dragged on and on I grew more desperate. Apart from everything else, the house needed work done on it and there was no way I could afford the repairs. One night I was so freaked out trying to think of someone I could turn to for help that I phoned Cosmopolitan magazine and demanded to speak to the editor. They had just published a glowing review of John's latest album, 'Glorious Fool' (1981) I think it was and I tried telling her my side of the story, hoping maybe that I'd get some helpful advice from her. I told her how he'd been violent to me and how I wasn't getting any proper royalties but all she gave me were platitudes about how I should get something out of the divorce and how I'd be able to make money playing again. It was extraordinary. I couldn't go public with my story because I didn't think anybody wanted to hear it then and I always had to bear in mind that he wasn't just my husband, he was the father of two children who loved him.

It's little wonder that in 1984 I finally went over the edge, identifying with the woman in Bob Dylan's song: "What's a sweetheart like you doing in a dump like this?" I was beginning to be overwhelmed by the reality of my situation.

It was in 1983 that someone brought me round the new Dylan album 'Infidels'. I couldn't believe how good it was, and how it seemed to be about me! "How much abuse can you take?" The breakdown started because I was so desperate to feel hope, to feel that someone out there knew what was happening. Few people from the music business bothered to check and see how we were, so when this record came along

I thought that Dylan was sending me coded messages through his songs. The album is full of Biblical and mythological references: "In another lifetime, she could have owned the world, faithfully wed to a righteous king who wrote psalms ..."and "You were born with a snake in both of your fists..." It touched me on the deepest levels, spiritual as well as emotional.

I began obsessing on things deep in my psyche, mystical things. In 1982 I had made a video of my song 'The Ancient Wisdom'. Art, Paul and I all met up for a reunion just after, in The Savoy Hotel in London of all places, and they were convinced I was going to get a deal with it, even wrote me letters of recommendation, but nothing came of it. I think that disappointment added to the stress. The song was very symbolic, drawing on Goddess imagery and the roots of ancient religion. I'd written it, but even I didn't fully understand the symbolism until years later I made a friend who had studied all this stuff and who helped me to understand that there had been millennia of Goddess worship long before anyone dreamt of a One God. These were similar themes to 'Infidels' and I became convinced that someone had shown Dylan my tape and he had written 'Infidels' in response.

I was so sad and ill that winter of '83. I had been traumatised. It was twenty years since I'd met John and what did I have to show for it? I felt so like nothing that I thought I had been privileged that this man had let me be his wife. I became anorexic – I felt I didn't deserve to eat; I slipped into depression. That Christmas I was working on an apple farm of all places, to try to get some pennies together when Dylan's film 'Renaldo and Clara' was shown on TV. When you are slipping into madness, everything seems to contain hidden messages, to magically relate to you.

Seeing the film took me back to the time when John and I had been in Jamaica and we'd met Perry Henzell, director of 'The Harder They Come'. He had just come from seeing the rushes of the Dylan film. I was dressed all in white with long flowing hair and Perry said I looked just like one of the women in the film, the character played by Joan Baez and Sarah, Dylan's wife.

I was taking all this stuff in and it was making me worse and worse. I began to think I was some sort of messianic figure. I took to my bed and stopped eating and drinking until I started hearing and seeing things. I had to get hold of a bible to understand all these messages that seemed to be coming to me. I felt I had to pray for the whole world, that I was sourcing something momentous. I was getting messages through the radio and I would sometimes chant through the night.

For six weeks I lay there thinking I was having some sort of divine revelation and what was happening to me would spread out into the world and save it. I wasn't looking at being saved myself. I was frightened because I still had a fear of God in me and I seemed to be some sort of witch. I had to keep washing myself to keep myself pure because I thought I was under some divine microscope. It was as if I knew all the secrets of the world, that I had stumbled on the inner workings of the Kabbala, the mystical teachings of Judaism.

I had never been into Tarot cards or anything like that, but I had bought my youngest son a pack as a game and now I wanted to see it and touch it. I pulled out a card. It was the Empress reversed; the same card as on the Dylan album sleeve. What did it mean? Was it black magic? What was happening? Was I a witch? It says in the Bible "Thou shalt not suffer a witch to live". Of course, we'd been with Witchseason Productions! It must have been bad karma. I started to sing 'I don't wanna know about evil'. Was I pagan? I was terrified of being burnt at the stake. Maybe it was in my genes? Maybe I had been burned in another life? I thought I was magic and I was purifying myself and helping the world in the process. It was horrifying.

In the middle of all this, my daughter had a birthday party. Some of her friends came up to my room to say "hello", and one of them noticed the card and told me her mother was into Tarot. When the mother came to pick her daughter up, she came upstairs and explained to me that upright the card meant 'a fruitful woman', but reversed means she's out of tune, out of sync, psychic alienation, all of which fed into the cauldron that was boiling up inside me.

Within days I started to have moments of catatonic inertia and I'd come back tripping out on something or other. I thought all the musicians in the world would come together to help the starving; I thought I could be inside Dylan's head, know what it was to be like him. I started burning up and found myself phoning Joe Boyd I was so scared at what was happening. "How are you, Bev?" "I'm spirit." "Spirit's got to eat too", went the conversation. He obviously gathered something was going seriously wrong because he promptly came down to Heathfield to see me. He found a house with no heating and no TV so he organised some money for us, bless him.

I was in bed for six weeks, in and out of reality, in and out of dream worlds and other worlds. I have always leaned towards the mystical and the 'other-worldly'. There had even been a night in Woodstock when I seemed to project a chakra onto a blank wall.[87]

It was about 3am in the morning. The most exquisite silver moth had landed on the kaftan I was wearing, like an ornate silver brooch, and I was just sitting there, feeling tired and staring at the white wall. It was just coming up to sunrise. I suddenly saw this spinning light on the wall. I said to John, "Can you see that?" and he said yes he could. I asked him where he thought it came from and he told me he thought I was projecting it. The last time we got together as a family, in the '90s, when even my eldest son was there, John told the children this story and the kids all went "wow" and "cool".

It wasn't 'wow' and 'cool' that night in Heathfield. I hadn't been eating or drinking properly for weeks and that's why I went off my head. I was finally taken to hospital on the night

---

[87]**Chakra.** A 'wheel of light' or energy centre, seven of which are supposedly located at different points in our bodies. From traditional Indian medicine.

of the full moon. I had been so high I thought I was going to explode and shoot to the moon. I had this little Egyptian box on my bedside table. It was full of sentimental treasures such as my children's milk teeth and an amber stone I'd collected from somewhere. I kept fiddling with it until my hand found this little golden toothpick I kept in there and I grabbed it and plunged it into the mattress; I realised later I had been trying to ground myself.

They kept me in the hospital for ten days, and I didn't wake up for the first three of them. I remember I was lying on a trolley with about ten doctors around. I suddenly crossed my arms on my chest and announced: "Israel is dying". "Exhale and lie down". "I can't breathe." I could feel myself floating through the ceiling looking down on the bed, telling myself to get back into my body and start breathing. I felt something being pushed into the sole of my foot, a needle perhaps, to check if I were dead. A voice said: "I can't feel a pulse." Suddenly I sat bolt upright. Two doctors went flying across the room. Then I heard another voice: "I hate it when they do that." I was alive.

Three days later, and what do I hear floating in through the window? 'The Chimes of Freedom Flashing.' I looked out and could see into the games room where there was a woman dressed in white, grooving to Dylan. Oh no, there was no getting away from him! At that moment I came back to my senses. I realised there was one of us in every town, a woman dressed in black or white, so desperate, so unhappy that, listening to Dylan, she believed he was singing directly to her. I looked at a bible by the bedside and in the flyleaf was written; "Property of Amberstone Hospital" and I thought, "My god, girl, you've really done it now!"[88]

The food in the hospital was so awful I refused to eat it and the staff thought there was some religious reason and offered

---

[88]**Amberstone.** East Sussex mental hospital.

me *kosher* food instead, which was equally as bad. At one point I was going round gathering up all the aerosol cans in the ward, saying how dangerous they were for the environment. And I'd never even heard of CFCs in those days![89] Eventually, having given me masses of Largactyl, an antipsychotic sedative, and made me drink loads of water, they let me go home.

---

[89] CFCs - Chlorofluorocarbons. Man-made CFCs are used as propellants in aerosols and are a main cause of holes in the ozone layer.

CHAPTER 8

Heathfield – Eastbourne – Brighton 1985-1998

When Joe Boyd had come to see how I was doing, he'd brought a friend with him, a woman who happened to be a disciple of Scientology. Scientologists don't accept the existence of mental illness and see medicines as poisons. No sooner had I got back from the hospital than this woman phoned me and advised me to stop taking any pills I was on. There are always people silly enough to do that, just as there are always people silly enough to listen to them. I didn't like the Largactyl, I felt it was slowing me down and I'd heard it could adversely affect your thyroid. Worse still, it was making me put on weight; I'd been trying to eat properly to keep myself from floating off like a hot air balloon, because of course I didn't want to get ill again, and the pounds were creeping on. So I listened to her and stopped taking it and everything seemed fine at first.

The trouble was I was not facing up to the reality that there really was something wrong with me, something that could reappear at any time. I was still tangled up in all the Dylan mythological stuff, and I couldn't shake off the thought that there was a reason for all I had been going through and eventually I would find out what that reason was. I started to read everything I could. Books seemed to come to me as if by magic and one book would lead to another.

One of the first that really got me going was 'Supernature' by Lyall Watson, which treated the supernatural as part of nature.[90] Colin Wilson's writings on the occult also affected me profoundly.[91] I read Robert Graves and began to learn about the White Goddess and the alphabet of the trees, which goes a long way back before anyone came up with the idea of there only being one god. In a Christian culture there's this superstitious belief that any kind of 'supernatural' gift you may have must come from black magic if it doesn't come from Jesus; even worse, it could be pagan. That was one of the fears that had infected me when I was ill. I learned there was nothing to fear about mystical experiences. Plants can feel, humans can sense, it's all part of nature.

I learned that witches had been 'wise women', not just evil-minded hags and that there was a long, long history of goddess worship and the accepted divinity of women, whatever that may mean, from all over the world. I learned that things are not always as they seem, that Shakespeare was right when he wrote: "There are more things in heaven and earth, Horatio, Than are dreamt of in your philosophy." From mythology I started getting into science, devouring books on anti-matter, protons, seemingly impossible things like electricity, which you can't actually see until you plug it in. I became fascinated by the idea of String Theory; maybe we are all living a multiverse, not a universe.

In one version of String Theory, known as M Theory, space/time enjoys 11 dimensions, as compared to the three plus time we accept today. These dimensions undulate close to us and to each other although we can't see them and things are measured by vibration, so that magic, madness and mysticism all vibrate at the same time. All this seemed to make great sense

---

[90]Lyall Watson (1939-2008) 'Supernature: A Natural History of the Supernatural'. Hodder Stoughton (1973)

[91]Colin Wilson (b1931) Philosopher and prolific writer on true crime and mysticism.

to me. If you have a belief system based on history, mythology and science then you can rest easy because it puts you in the picture of what you are, which is just a speck of dust. We all think we're so important and yet we may well be just an offshoot of indifferent natural processes. Such a belief system explains away this need some of us have for a godhead and helps us to understand that what will be will be and all we have to do is accept it as human beings. I believe we need to recognise that we are the caretakers of this planet and every child has a right to live and sleep in peace and safety. Until we get that right we haven't achieved anything. It doesn't matter where we've been in space, the money hasn't gone to the right place.

Learning all these truths seemed to help me to get better. I was getting stronger all the time, and the fact that I wasn't taking any medication didn't seem to matter. What I see now is that I wasn't really keeping myself grounded properly, that sooner or later, I could have another breakdown.

Art Garfunkel came to visit me at this time and I remember his saying: "What's it all about, Bev?" And I told him I thought I'd had an attack of 'Dylanitis'. "Yeah", he drawled, "I think a lot of people are getting it. I think Paul had it until he met him in person and now he's alright!" He went on to say that perhaps I should meet Dylan now since John hadn't given me the chance, but I said no because I knew I was in no shape to be meeting people like that.

I was very aware that Artie was watching me all weekend, but we had a good time and he enjoyed playing with the children. I remember I cooked turkey and brown rice and he loved it. He was very sweet and offered me some money before he left, but I couldn't take it. However, he'd obviously realised the seriousness of the situation, and some money arrived from him after he'd gone; I was very grateful.

The divorce had dragged on for ten years. When I finally did get my settlement, which was the house, I had to pay off the mortgage myself. Much as I loved living in Kenana, I really couldn't keep the place together and it needed a hell of a lot of work done to it. I thought that by selling up I could clear all my debts and have enough left over to start afresh somewhere else. I realised that it wouldn't fetch as much as it would if I could've done all the necessary repairs and redecoration but nobody told me that if you got planning permission, you could pull down a house like that and replace it with two others and make a killing. So I sold it for about £130,000, which was on the low side, and somebody else made the killing. After all my debts had been paid off, there was just £80,000 left to set up anew in a three-bed-roomed terraced house in Eastbourne. John got away scot free, financially speaking.

There was one curious event before we left Heathfield.

In 1987, Dylan was playing at Wembley Arena and I went to see the show. He sang 'Blowing in the Wind' and that night the worst storm for 284 years hit Britain. That's the sort of coincidence that strange fantasies can be weaved from. It had stormed the night I met him in Woodstock and it stormed the night I saw him in London. Is it any wonder he figured so prominently in my madness? Makes you wonder what would have happened if we could have ever spent any time together.

So in 1989 I moved to Eastbourne. We had been in the country so long, we really were country bumpkins. The new house didn't have much of a garden, but there was the beach nearby. I chose Eastbourne because my teenage kids were always trying to get there on a Saturday. There were shops, cinemas, discos, all the things youngsters enjoy. My eldest son was at college there too, so it seemed the best place to go. But I didn't know many people there, so I spent a lot of my time ferrying my youngest son and myself back and forth to Heathfield. I knew people in Chiddingly who had been really supportive to me all through the divorce and after. I have never lost touch with long-time friend Sam Heaphy. Over the years we've written many songs together and he and his wife Moira have always been there for me.

I had been lucky to have this lovely house in the country for so long, and I really missed sitting in the garden, getting inspired or tootling round the country lanes in my old banger, visiting nice little pubs. But in Eastbourne I started doing the odd local gig and then going up to perform in small folk clubs in London. I thought I could salvage my career, that someone would want to make an album with me. But it proved impossible. This was the '80s, the music world had changed. Keyboards with electronic beats were in, acoustic guitar-playing singer/songwriters were out. It was all house music, Indie bands, New Romantics and work-out tapes!

In the middle of all this, John came and spent Christmas 1991 with us. His then partner, Annie, had left him and he was very distressed and drinking far too much. He loved her, but treated her really badly, perhaps as badly as he'd treated me. The kids were worried about him and asked me if he could join us that year as he had nowhere else to go. I never thought I'd do this, but I said yes, on the condition that he brought another man with him, someone who would be there to make sure he behaved himself. He agreed to this because I think he wanted to come back to what he thought of as his family and so we spent our first Christmas together for years.

It didn't take long for me to realise that he'd stashed a bottle of Bacardi in the fridge and he would pop into the kitchen, down a quick glass, then come back and finish whatever he was doing. When we went shopping for a turkey and all the trimmings or other goodies for Christmas, he'd spot a pub and say, "Let's pop in there", and proceed to down double or triple Bacardis with beer chasers. It was ridiculous; I thought he was intent on killing himself. We managed to get through the festive season without any quarrels and then he asked me if I thought we could get back together if he gave up the drink.

I told him we'd have a much better chance if he did but I couldn't make any promises there and then. If he could have stopped drinking and having those fits of violence, we could've had some sort of normal life together. The kids would've loved us to try again, but there was no way I could let a man who drank like that back into my life. I told him he had an enormous problem with alcohol and he would die if he didn't stop. He was on his best behaviour that Christmas but I didn't really believe he could change. He looked like a man determined to destroy himself – he was overweight, bloated, his beautiful turquoise eyes had lost their sparkle and were all bloodshot. You can't live around someone who's on such a self-destructive path, watching them die in front of your eyes.

Things could have been done to save him, there were enough big strong men around to drag him kicking and screaming to rehab, but I couldn't do it. He wasn't going to take his last drink in my kitchen! I had seen through this great musician who created beautiful music and knew him for what he was - a big kid who never faced up to responsibility, who hid behind the booze. I know the children would have liked us to get together again, but that was never going to happen unless he gave up the drink. I did, however, agree to do some gigs with him in Putney in the early '90s.

We didn't sing together – I was the supporting act - but he would insist that we walked into the gig side by side, maybe so that the band could see us and wonder if there was anything rekindling between us. The gigs went well, but on the last night, at about 4 a.m., he came banging on my hotel room door, calling for me: "Beverley, Beverley, wake up. I want to talk to you." I went straight into panic mode again. Fortunately my daughter was staying in the same room as me. She got up and told him where to go in no uncertain terms, as only a daughter can.

We were in Eastbourne for about four years. My eldest son got a job in a restaurant and then moved abroad; my daughter was with me sometimes but went off travelling round America while my youngest had started to work for his dad as a sound engineer, so he was backwards and forwards. I saw John yet again when my daughter asked me to go and keep an eye on him while she was in the States. He had agreed to do some gigs in The Channel Islands but he wasn't in good health. For my daughter's sake, I agreed and spent an amicable few days watching the gigs and hanging out with the band, but when

John asked me to go and spend a few days with just him on the Island of Sark, I couldn't do it. I felt safe enough while other people were around, but I wasn't prepared to spend any time alone with him. That was the last time I ever saw him.

I still couldn't find regular employment as a musician and by 1993 I was existing on Social Security again. I found it impossible to make ends meet so eventually I had to borrow £5000 from the bank just to keep ticking over. When I couldn't pay it back, the bank insisted I sell the house, even though it was a relatively small sum I owed them. Unfortunately, this coincided with the crash in the housing market and I ended up having to accept about £34,000 for a house I'd paid £70,000 cash for. When I'd paid off the bank and various other expenses, I didn't even have enough left to put down a deposit on a flat and live at the same time, so I had to start renting. That's when we moved to Brighton, well Hove, actually, as they say.

With the help of a friend, I found a great flat on the seafront overlooking Hove lawns where we stayed for the next six or so years. I could see the sea crashing from my window and watch the moon over the ocean. Brighton is a great place for musicians and I was hopeful I would at least be able to find some good people to play with. But it was in Brighton, bohemian city that it is, that I began to realise the full extent of my youngest son's problems.

When he was sixteen, he had started working with John as his sound engineer, though every time he came back from a stint, he would declare, "I can't stand it. I'm never going there again." He had always longed to see his father, he loved him and thought he was amazing but spending time with him turned out to be a rude awakening.

Every boy needs a role model; unfortunately John was a hard-drinking hell-raiser with some very shady friends, all of whom would play little games on our son to try and harden him up and initiate him into their sort of 'man's world'. It was difficult for the boy. He'd been brought up in the country by a loving mother and now he saw the reality of how his father really was. With a role model determined to get off his face as often as he could, my sensitive young son began to learn some very bad habits. Of course, there were fun times too.

He came back once after working with John in Scotland sometime in 2001 and told me how his father had decided to put on a kilt for the first time in years. They had a taxi waiting because they had to go to the recording studio. The driver was a friend, 70-year-old Ian McMinn, who came into the house to see what was keeping them and found John stark bollock naked while they were trying to pin this kilt round him. They eventually got to the studio where at one point John sat in the chair used by the technician. As he swivelled round in it, it fell backwards and the kilt suddenly flew up over his head. I would like to say here that John never owned a pair of underpants in all the time I knew him. Apparently he just laughed off the incident and went on with the recording.

All this time I was going through health problems of my own. The years of stress and palpitations had culminated in my being diagnosed as having hyper-tension. I was prescribed beta blockers to take when I was performing and they seemed to work well. I was managing to do more small gigs, but my son seemed to be around all the time and money and jewellery kept going missing until I began to think I was going crazy again. Finally I felt so drained by what was happening that I ended up at my doctor's in tears. I couldn't talk to her about anything, so she gave me a prescription for Seroxat and told me I had to start taking that.

Seroxat is a very interesting drug. Its active ingredient is Paroxetine, which is a type of anti-depressant known as a selective serotonin reuptake inhibitor, sometimes known as a 'happy pill'. For the first three months, I just wanted to read books and stay up all night. It felt good, so I didn't worry about it, just sent off for my repeat prescriptions. I rarely saw the doctor but that didn't seem to matter. I noticed I suddenly had a lot of confidence, which was a good thing.

I began gigging again, both in Brighton and in London, even running a regular 'open mike' night for singer/songwriters at the Gladstone in Brighton, which became very popular. I played at some blues festivals and even did a few spots with my old boyfriend, Bert Jansch, who by now was an ageing man with a heart by-pass and a string of ex-wives and children to support. The Seroxat makes you feel you're on top of things, that you can go out and face the world and not get uptight and paranoid that people are thinking you're just a flaky folk singer. I could get up on a stage with 60 or 70 pissed-up people bunched up in front of me and talk to them with ease, make them laugh. It's the sort of drug that might have helped Nick when he was alive, at least for a while.

Sometimes I would get so high playing that I would leave my guitar at the Gladstone and walk home alone through the streets of Brighton at 2am in the morning, itself a crazy thing to do. It was a better feeling than sex! What sex? There was no sex. You don't feel like sex on Seroxat. No matter how many gorgeous young men came up and looked longingly into my eyes, I had no idea what they were on about. So many missed opportunities...

With Seroxat, life's problems seem to flow away like water off a duck's back but they don't really disappear. Underneath, I still had an uneasy awareness that something not right was going on with my youngest. I got into a habit of scratching my head until it bled and that would make me feel better. I had developed psoriasis of the scalp and I suspect it was by-product of the Seroxat. The scratching was a form of self-abuse I suppose and one that I still indulge in today when I get stressed, but it was when I started to puke regularly that I decided it was time to come off the pills.

I'd been on them for about five years and coming off was ugly. I had nightmares and would sometimes scream in the night. I was shaking and had hot and cold sweats. I would vomit and not know why I was vomiting. I couldn't sleep and would spend hours sitting at the window, staring out to sea, almost catatonic. I didn't want to face reality, even though I knew I had to. Things people said would upset me because they were true and I didn't want to face truths, especially not about my baby.

I think I was in shock, consumed with fear about what was happening to my boy, how he was getting into heavier and heavier drugs, and I couldn't help him or control him. Watching your child deteriorate before your eyes and knowing that the father he adores is at least in part responsible for this darkness is a burden I wouldn't wish any parent to bear. He had developed an attitude and looked and talked like he came from a black ghetto. I couldn't handle it. My sweet young skateboarder had turned into this shifty person who lied to me and who stole from me to fund his growing heroin habit.

Nothing was really happening career wise, either. The impetus the Seroxat had given me was draining away. There were one or two good moments though. Through Richard Clayton, who'd been a good buddy of mine for about fifteen years, I got back in touch with Jeff Dexter, a DJ who'd managed a band called America and had been a good friend of Marc Bolan's.[92] He got me a half hour spot on the Bob Harris Radio Show. I did two songs live on the show, 'Friends and Lovers' was one and the other was 'Potter's Blues', a new song I was still working on. Then we talked about my life with John. After the programme had aired, Bob said he thought I'd been 'very kind' to John in the interview.

I did some good work with Nick Pynn, a string man who can play fiddle, banjo, guitar, dulcimer and mandocello.[93] I also enjoyed playing with Frank O'Shea, the bass player, but we

---

[92]**America** - Anglo-American folk rock band who came to prominence in the early '70s. **Marc Bolan** (1947-1977) English singer/songwriter and guitarist and founder of T. Rex, psychedelic folk-rock acoustic group who were trailblazers for the glam rock movement.

[93]**Dulcimer** - also known as 'mountain dulcimer'and 'Appalachian dulcimer' - a stringed instrument with frets, played by plucking. **Mandocello** – stringed instrument similar to a lute, also played by plucking.

only ever managed to do one gig together. No-one was offering me any studio time. I paid for Nick Pynn and myself to lay down a couple of tracks together; fortunately I haven't lost that master tape in all the upheavals that followed.

Another good thing that happened at this time was the reunion of The Levee Breakers sometime in 1996 or '97. (Unfortunately, I've never been one to keep a diary, so sometimes I get a bit hazy about dates.) Johnny Joyce had caught up with me playing a gig in Bunjie's Folk Cellar, a famous old blues venue from the '60s and he then wrote to me that people had been saying they wanted to see us do a reunion gig and asking me if I was interested. I couldn't say no to that. It was a joy to be playing with him again. We played The Cabbage Patch in Twickenham with Davey Graham as support. I remember Davey played classical guitar standing up, wearing a suit and a Spanish hat. Ralph McTell and Don Partridge came along that night and it really was like taking a loop in time. We played another gig for the Tunbridge Wells festival. Geoff Bradford joined us there. In 1962 Geoff had been head-hunted by Brian Jones for his new band, The Rolling Stones, but he hadn't stayed with them for long because he thought they were too commercial for his liking, and he was a blues man through and through.

Unfortunately we couldn't play many more live gigs because Johnny couldn't handle performing any more, he was getting too fragile and nervy. I managed to spend quite a lot of time with him before he died in 2004, but sadly we never managed to do any more recording together. Mind you, he always had a tape recorder going when we were thrashing numbers out, so perhaps with the wonders of technology I'll be able to record with him again one day... He was a great guitarist and he had such a special sound.

CHAPTER 9

Brighton – Hove 1998-2009

All my dreams and hopes were falling apart again. By 1998 I was doing gigs and not getting paid for them, not even by Bert Jansch, who'd fallen out with his agent and wasn't getting paid himself! If I did a paying gig, the musicians I used would sit around drinking all the money away. My health was deteriorating and I was too preoccupied and worried about my youngest son to keep on top of things. I finally lost my home because everything was just going over my head. I couldn't bring myself to read my mail and I had no idea what was happening, that I had run into rent arrears and was supposed to go to court to sort it out. My poor daughter was up and down from London trying to look after things for me, but she couldn't keep the house of cards from falling down. It all culminated in the bailiffs arriving one day in 1999 to evict me and my not even knowing they were due.

For the next six months I had to live in one room in a half-way house before being moved to a flat in Oriental Place, Brighton. It was here that I finally had to accept the full extent of my son's addiction.

I have always felt an affinity for the phoenix, the mythical fire-bird that lives for a thousand years, then builds a nest of myrrh leaves on which it burns to death and then rises again from its own ashes.

In Oriental Place I was in the ashes of my life to date. It seemed it had all gone – the career, the marriage, the money, my house, so many little treasures collected over a lifetime disappearing day by day.

But ironically, when you are at your lowest that's when good things can start to happen. I wasn't doing any gigging at this time, but I did manage to record my first album since 'Road to Ruin' – 'No Frills'. No frills indeed - we did it on a shoestring in a friend's flat, but with the help of my son's mixing skills it turned out a good album and I'm proud of it, and of the fact it's still out there circulating. That was a phoenix moment. But all the time, I was having to deal with my poor son's drug abuse.

It must be so hard for boys who have a famous father who ultimately becomes a bad influence on them and I have always tried to be as supportive as I can, but sometimes there has to be 'tough love' or you go down with the ship. It was a Titanic moment there in Oriental Place - he was in and out of trouble and the police finally advised me that the best thing I could do was move and not give him the forwarding address.

It's one of the hardest things I've ever had to do, but I took that advice because however much you love your child, if what they are doing drives you to the brink of destruction, you have to save yourself. So after three years, I left Oriental Place.

With my daughter's help, I managed to find a studio flat deeper into Hove and settled there hoping for some peace and sanity to rebuild myself. I was shattered. My health had deteriorated and I was diagnosed with Diabetes Type Two. It took them so long to find out what was wrong with me, that I suffered organ damage before the diagnosis came through. But at least I was beginning to sort things out in my head until the day I ran into my son and he promised me he was off the drug. I was so happy to hear that, I immediately let him back into my life - and my flat. The road to hell is paved with good intentions, and a junkie's road is more cluttered than most.

To be fair to him, he did manage to stay clean for quite a while until the next time he went to stay with his father. He found John looking very yellow and suggested he might have jaundice. John said he didn't think he had, but the very next day when they'd gone to the hospital for him to have a check-up, the nurse took one look at him and declared: "Jaundice" in no uncertain terms. John's liver and pancreas were damaged by the years of self-abuse and I believe he may also have been somewhat diabetic. My son came home completely distraught by his father's condition and just fell back into his old drug habit.

This was the situation when, in 2002, I was approached by the BBC to take part in a programme they were planning entitled 'John Martyn: Johnny Too Bad'. John was about to have his right leg amputated for 'infected cysts.' Knowing him as well as I did, I always believed the cysts were formed in a bottle but I was happy to participate in the programme, although forever churning up old memories can be unsettling, especially when you're not particularly well yourself.

John phoned me just before he had the operation. He started the call by singing: "See that my grave is kept clean" then asked me if I thought he was going to die. I told him we were all going to die soon and he'd probably outlive us all. Then he said: "I'm going to have my leg off tomorrow. Do you forgive me?" I told him I forgave him but he had to forgive himself. He said he couldn't. I tried to convince him that having the leg off would save his life and the rest of it was up to him, the drinking and the drugs. I tried to keep the tone of the conversation light, even cracking jokes to make him laugh. He always laughed at my 'wicked' sense of humour. That's how we ended the call. We never spoke again.

By 2006 my son was battling his old demons again and my health took a downward turn. I wasn't performing or writing much, so I was delighted when Fatboy Slim chose to include 'Primrose Hill', one of my tracks from 'Road to Ruin', on his album 'Palookaville' in 2006.[94] At the same time I was also

---

[94]Fatboy Slim (b1963) Real name Norman Cook. British DJ, musician record producer and pioneer of electronic dance music.

featured in a long article in The Observer newspaper, and it felt good to get some recognition again; it had been a while. Unfortunately, 'Palookaville' wasn't one of Fatboy's most successful albums and my moment of rekindled glory passed as quickly as it came.

There were days when it seemed that the best day of my life that I could remember to that point had been in 1988, when I had got the money from the sale of Kenana and gone on my only holiday for twenty years. It was so nice being able to do something like that, like a normal person. It had made me feel like a millionaire and I'd loved every minute of it. No wonder I was so sad and vulnerable if that was my best memory to date.

Then out of the blue I received a letter from Matt Deighton asking me to go and do a gig at his club The Barley Wheel, in London. Matt is a guitarist/songwriter who used to play with a jazz funk band called Mother Earth. He's a very good guitarist who stood in for Noel Gallagher on Oasis' 2001 tour and he'd also played with Paul Weller. I knew his reputation as a musician so I agreed to go up there and perform. The evening went down so well that he invited me back to do a gig with him. It was great. Here I was, playing again with a man who seemed to be on the same wavelength.

When we played, it was as if he knew instinctively what I was doing with the music and he would improvise accordingly. It's such a marvellous feeling when that sort of connection happens, I threw myself into it whole-heartedly. We did a few gigs together and a bit of recording, and then we took to getting together at his place in Essex, where we would play and try to write songs together.

It had been the connection through the music that had been so powerful between John and myself, and here was another man I felt I could create good music with. Boundaries began to get blurred. We got very, very high when we played together. Matt seemed to be an answer to a prayer, and inevitably we got closer and closer. I don't think I'm giving any secrets away when I say that as I got to know him, I learned that he suffered from bi-polar disorder – he was a manic depressive. I was so beset by the problems with my son, which were getting worse and worse again that I let myself escape into this romantic dream of being able to recapture what it means to be making music with someone you love. Matt and I went off on one together – over the moon, as they say. I began to obsess about The Phoenix and the Turtle, a long, allegorical poem by Shakespeare about the death of ideal love. I stopped thinking about eating or taking my medication; I was winging on my mystical way again.

Of course I was bound to come crashing down sooner or later because what goes up must come down and my blood sugar levels were all over the place. Fortunately I was at home with a friend when I began to suffer from some sort of diabetic fit in which I kept falling over and banging my head, but I was also talking strangely. Some people can get away with behaviour like that, but I'm glad my friend called an ambulance and I was taken to the hospital. The doctor there examined me and decided I should be hospitalised, at least for observation. So I was transferred to the local mental hospital, Mill View, and stayed there for the next five weeks or so.

It was interesting to experience mental health care over an extended period of time. There were so many people in there suffering from drug-related problems, particularly young people who had been taking Ecstasy and smoking too much Skunk, that particularly nasty, genetically modified strain of marijuana. I also noticed there seemed to be a lot of Jewish people in there – Red Sea pedestrians, as I fondly called them - with similar problems to mine. This made me think that our mental illness could be hereditary, caused by the old tradition of marrying cousins to cousins, which keeps the money, if not the senses, in the family. I mentioned this to the psychiatrist, but I don't think he was overly impressed with my analysis.

The thing about the hospital treatment is that you have to stick to their routine. I wasn't diagnosed with bi-polar disorder or anything specific that time, but I had to play by the rules – breakfast, lunch and dinner like clockwork, then heavy sedation at 10pm and off to sleep. If, like me, you tried to buck the system and stay awake, they would descend on you as a team and forcibly sedate you. I know they didn't like doing it, but they did it anyway. Sometimes it was the only way to stop a patient who wasn't eating or sleeping from burning themselves out.

This sort of institutionalised existence can quickly become a habit and adjusting to life back outside can be problematical. You want to revert to the regime all the time, because it's safe and comfortable but for a creative person it's a living death because it destroys your creativity.

But this time I realised I had to keep taking my medication until I was completely stable again. That was vital. Twice I had been overwhelmed by illness and that was enough for one lifetime. It's only when you're mobile and out in the world that you can meet people. And if I wanted to sing again, I needed to be out in the world.

As you get older you don't do it so much, and starting again becomes even more difficult if you've had a gap in your career and people don't know where you are. Illness adds to the problems. But the most important thing is that you have to get healed, there's no hope at all unless you can do that, no matter how long it takes. Without healing, you'll never have a good relationship; you'll keep repeating the same mistakes until you die. Life becomes too painful, you don't know how to live it and your confidence vanishes.

There have been times when I couldn't even pick up a phone to ring anybody, too afraid that the way they would speak to me would make me feel like I was nothing again. Because in the music business, there are always some people who will do that to you and I knew from experience what a terrible feeling that is. But that was then and this is now. It may not be easy, because first you have to recognise and admit that you need healing and then you have to give it the time it takes.

Healing isn't always a quick process. When we've suffered a lot of pain and turmoil it can take a long time to recover. Each of us can only go at the pace that works for us. Sometimes, unless someone tells you, you may not even know there's help out there or how to access that help and you walk around wounded and hurt for years, not able to do the work you were born for, your gift in life. Life becomes a round of drudgery as you wake up every morning to the same problems, the cooking, the laundry, the looking after a damaged man-child. There never seems a way of getting back to a place where you can burst into a day, full of expectation and enthusiasm. But there is. Sometimes it happens through talking therapies, sometimes through taking the right medication, sometimes through love, through friendship, however it happens you know you have the rest of your life to look forward to, in the best meaning of those words. I finally faced up to the fact that Bob Dylan hadn't written an album for me. I'd been totally obsessed with him because I was ill. Thank the gods I was too sick to stalk him! At the same time, I was denying the fact that I was part of the John and Beverley Martyn myth, and that my ex-husband had written songs about me, songs that were good, songs that his fans love to this day.

It is in our songs that we tell our story. I may have taken some wrong turns in life and put my faith in the wrong people, but no matter what has happened to me over the years, I have never lost my gift for music and I wasn't going to lose it now. This phoenix would rise again, but not if I rushed her.

By 2008 life had begun to change for the better. My son was attempting to detox again, which is not the easiest of jobs in a town filled with dopers and dealers, and I moved again, to a lovely one-bed roomed flat right behind The Old Market Arts Centre in the Brunswick area of Brighton. I'd always felt at home in that area and I sensed that being surrounded by musicians and poets would help me start playing again. I bided my time, getting stronger and stronger.

Within a year I had a call from an old friend, Chris Hill. I've known him since the Sixties, but we lost track of each other for a long time. He used to run a bookshop and gallery called Indica, which was where John Lennon first met Yoko Ono. He is very friendly with Denny Lane and I knew Denny from the '60s when we'd both had the same manager and had even been flatmates for a time. Denny had given me my first guitar, a classic Spanish acoustic, and once I'd managed to get round that OK, he lent me an amazing Rickenbacker, a top notch American electric guitar.

He was such a lovely little guy and he never changed; he was forever the Brummie, the gypsy boy. He'd found fame with The Moody Blues then went on to co-found Wings, with Paul McCartney, and together they wrote 'Mull of Kintyre'. I hadn't seen him for years because he'd been working a lot in America. Now something had happened with his visa when he'd left the States for some reason and he couldn't get back in, even though his wife was in Las Vegas, so he was based in the UK for a while.

Chris phoned me to say that Denny was in town on the 24th of January 2009 and I just had to go and see him play at The Old Market Art's Centre, literally outside my front door. Of course I went.

When Denny and I saw each other in the bar we fell into each other's arms and hugged for England as only two old survivors can hug. He was playing that night with Alan Thompson, the bass player from John Martyn's band and it was good to see him too.

The gig got underway and they were playing all the old hits, when he suddenly started playing one of my songs, 'Can't Get The One I Want'. He began to sing, then stopped and addressed the audience. "This was written by a girl in the Sixties called Beverley and I believe she's here. Come on, Bev." He called me up on the stage and I sang the rest of the song with them. It was great. The audience seemed to love it and they clapped and cheered and I felt really proud of myself. I could still do it! I still had the magic in me.

It was a beautiful thing for Denny to have done and just what I needed to kick start me into singing again. I handled myself well that night and after the gig Denny and I talked about getting together again for a bigger gig. I went home with wings on my feet. I knew at that moment that the phoenix was flying again.

One week later came the news of John's death.

EPILOGUE *Hove 2010*

I was married to John for ten years. It took another ten years to divorce him. It's taken more than ten years to recover from it all but I survived and feel stronger in my spirit now than I ever have before. Wisdom only comes with experience and experience only comes with age. I don't hate John for what he did to me because I know he was a damaged man. I don't even hate myself for not getting out sooner because I was damaged too. I think we both did the best we could but sadly, that just wasn't enough to keep us together as a family, however great the music we played together. John's death saddened me because he should have lived longer but I'm still here and my son's in rehab so there really is a tomorrow to look forward to.

I'm very lucky that my voice is as good as it's ever been. My fingertips are a bit soft because that's what happens when you stop performing and don't play guitar regularly but I've already started working on them again. The wonderful thing about music is that it stops the moment and enables you to transcend the bad things in your life. 'You can't keep a good woman down' is the title of one of the songs I co-wrote recently and I really believe that. I intend to never let anyone keep me down ever again so don't be surprised if you wake up one morning and hear this phoenix singing its heart out. She's been silent for too long.

Beverley aged 7 or 8

Captain of school netball team c1960

THE DECCA RECORD COMPANY LIMITED

proudly announces the launching of
its first new label for British product since 1929 :

DERAM RECORDS

We want you to meet our exciting new singles artists :

BEVERLEY *and* **CAT STEVENS**

and Producers :

Denny Cordell, Mike Hurst and Paul Samwell-Smith

and hear "The Velvet Touch of Johnny Howard" L.P.

at 18 Gt. Marlborough Street, W.1
on Monday, 26 September, from 5.30 - 7.0 p.m.

Enquiries : Tony Hall
REGent 2103
Press Office
RELiance 8111

Admission by invitation only.

Official invitation to the launch party for Deram Records 1966

It is because of the artists listed below that the festival had to happen. It was their generosity that made it possible for us to hold up a mirror and reflect their strength and integrity, their love and their music. We thank them all, not only for appearing, but for making everything so easy. **Eric Burdon and The Animals | The Association The Beach Boys | Beverly | Big Brother & The Holding Company | The Blues Project | Booker T & The MG's | Buffalo Springfield | Paul Butterfield Blues Band | The Byrds | Canned Heat | Country Joe & The Fish | Electric Flag | Grateful Dead | Jimi Hendrix Experience | The Impressions Jefferson Airplane | The Mamas and Papas | Hugh Masekela | Scott McKenzie | Steve Miller Blues Band | Moby Grape | Laura Nyro | The Paupers Quicksilver Messenger Service | Lou Rawls | Otis Redding | Johnny Rivers | Ravi Shankar | Simon and Garfunkel | Dionne Warwick | The Who**

Photocopy of flyer for the Monterey Pop Festival 1967

CIRCUS ALPHA CENTAURI

PRESENTS

AT THE ROUNDHOUSE

FOR YOUR ENTERTAINMENT AND PLEASURE

A CHRISTMAS FESTIVAL

OF MUSIC, SOUNDS, COLOUR, FILM, LIGHT, POETRY AND A BAZAAR
WITH ART-WORKS, SCULPTURE, FOOD, AND ALL SORTS OF TREASURES FOR PURCHASE

FROM WEDNESDAY DEC 20 - SUNDAY DEC 24, 6PM - 2AM EACH NIGHT
SUNDAY 5PM - 11PM

FEATURING

Wednesday dec 20

A Kaleidoscope of Word Music:
PETE BROWN AND THE POETRY BAND, THE LIVERPOOL SCENE,
TOM PICKARD AND THE LIVING MYTHOLOGY, GILLIAN BROWN, ROB COBBING, LEE HARWOOD,
SPIKE HAWKINS, LIBBY HOUSTON, ALAN JACKSON, TED MILTON, JEFF NUTTAL,
STUART MONTGOMERY, CARLYLE REEDY, PETE ROCHE,
RICHARD SYLVESTER
COMPERED BY JOHN PEEL
Tickets: 15/- (with seat); 10/-

Thursday dec 21

Blues
DANNY THOMPSON, AL STEWART, DORIS HENDERSON, SEBASTIAN JOURGENSEN, TIM WALKER,
WITH THE FIRST SHOWING OF BOB DYLAN'S MOVIE,
ALSO THE UNREHEARSED FILM OF MICK JAGGER, AND FILM OF THE
MONTEREY POP FESTIVAL AND NEWPORT JAZZ FESTIVAL . . . WITH BERT JANSCZ,
JOHN RENBOURN, JACQUI TERRY
Tickets: 15/- (with seat); 10/-

Friday dec 22

Psycho Circus
WITH CHRISTOPHER LOGUE, JOHN ARDEN, ADRIAN MITCHELL,
CARTOON ARCHETYPICAL SLOGAN THEATRE, GINGER JOHNSON AND HIS AFRICAN DRUMMERS,
WEST INDIAN STEEL BAND, ONE ANONYMOUS POP GROUP FROM BRIGHTON,
JACOU LIND
Tickets: 15/- (with seat); 10/-

Saturday dec 23

Pop Music, Film, Light
WITH THE FREEDOM, THE ANIMALS, DENNY LAINE, ZOOT MONEY & DANTALIAN'S CHARIOT,
THE FAIRPORT CONVENTION, BEVERLY, PANIC . . .
COMPERED BY JIMI HENDRIX
Tickets: £1 (with seat); 10/-

Sunday dec 24

A Night of Total Music and Incredible Films
IN TOTAL FREEDOM: WITH ARAB MUSICIANS, INDIAN MUSIC, JAZZ, BLUES
AND OTHER MUSIC (ARTISTES' NAMES CANNOT BE REVEALED)
Tickets at 15/-
Tickets each night: 15/- (inc. seats) or 10/-. Entrance for all five nights: £2 15s. 0d. Booking in advance from:
Circus Alpha Centauri, 6 Mason's Yard, Duke Street, St. James's, London, W.1. Telephone: WHITEHALL 1424

The Roundhouse will be heated!

* Chalk Farm.

" THE BEES SEEK OUT THE HONEY
WHILE THE FLIES SEEK OUT THE FILTH " — RUMMI
Printed at a fantastic speed DAVID OSLER & FRANK LTD. EU's 8733
Produced by CHRIS HILL; Ass Victoria and Lousia Ormsby-Gore
Thursday also COUNTRY JOE & THE FISH, THE INCREDIBLE STRING BAND
Stop all Film material of Thursday will be shown on Sunday only. Saturday and Sunday
from California AL COOPER WITH THE BLOOD, SWEAT AND TEARS,
ALSO BIG BROTHER AND THE HOLDING COMPANY, THE DOORS

Flyer for The Round House, London 1967

Beverley in 1968. Photographer: Unknown

John, Beverley and the children c1971. Photographer: Unknown

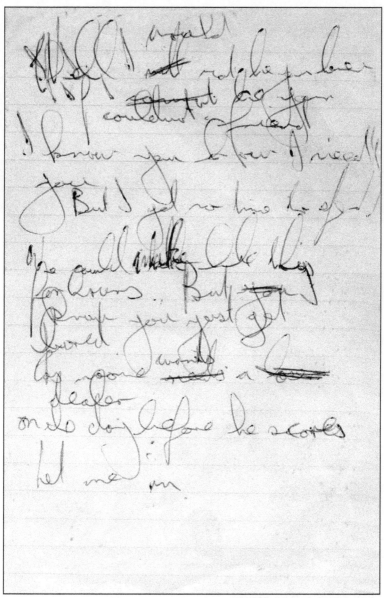

Lyrics to 'The Dealer' in John Martyn's handwriting. C 1974

Beverley and son Spenser at Chris Blackwell's house in Nassau 1976.
Photographer: John Martyn

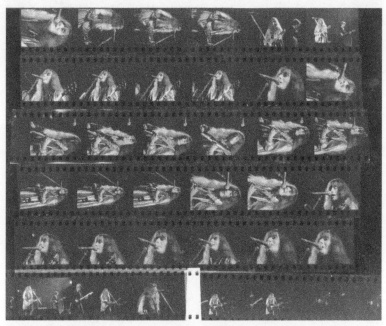

With Simon Climie on Loudon Wainwright tour c1980

With Nick Pynn at the Twelve Bar Club, London 1995

The Levee Breakers reunion gig. Tunbridge Wells c 1996

Lightning Source UK Ltd.
Milton Keynes UK
UKHW011823230321
380868UK00001B/129